IMPLEMENTING THE MATHEMATICS
NATIONAL CURRICULUM

IMPLEMENTING THE MATHEMATICS NATIONAL CURRICULUM

POLICY, POLITICS AND PRACTICE

Edited by
David C. Johnson and Alison Millett

P·C·P

Paul Chapman
Publishing Ltd

Paul Chapman Publishing Ltd
144 Liverpool Road
London
N1 1LA

British Library Cataloguing in Publication Data

Implementing the mathematics National Curriculum : policy,
politics and practice. – (New Bera dialogues)
1. Mathematics – Study and teaching (Elementary) – Great
Britain 2. Mathematics – Study and teaching (Secondary) –
Great Britain
I. Johnson, David C. (David Carlton), 1936- II. Millett,
Alison
375.5'1'0941
ISBN 1853963275

Typeset by Dorwyn Ltd
Printed and bound in Great Britain

A B C D E F G H 9 8 7 6

CONTENTS

TABLES

FIGURES

GENERAL EDITOR'S PREFACE

This is the first book to be published in the new series *New BERA Dialogues*, and it reflects very well the aims of the series as a whole.

Fostering educational research of high quality and demonstrating the value of good educational research to as wide an audience as possible are among the British Educational Research Association's primary purposes. This series is one way in which BERA seeks to achieve these purposes. Each book in the series will bring together a collection of papers reporting or discussing research on a particular aspect of education. The research reported will be of consistently high quality, both in itself and in its usefulness for informing constructive and critical thinking on matters of educational importance.

I am delighted to have *Implementing the Mathematics National Curriculum* as the first book in the new series. It demonstrates very clearly how careful and thoughtful research of various kinds can make a major contribution to the consideration of educational policy and practice.

Donald McIntyre

NOTES ON THE CONTRIBUTORS

Mike Askew is a Lecturer in Mathematics Education with particular interest in the teaching and learning of mathematics in primary schools. He has been active in the provision of 20-day inservice courses for teachers, with particular attention given to the implementation of Ma1, Using and Applying Mathematics across the mathematics curriculum. He is currently conducting research in the teaching and learning of numeracy.

Margaret Brown is a Professor of Mathematics Education and Head of the School of Education. Through her leadership role in research and development projects, national working groups, and professional associations (she is a past President of the Mathematical Association and currently is Chairperson of the Joint Mathematical Council, JMC), she has had the opportunity to participate directly in the process of negotiation and decision-making throughout the period of debate and final implementation of the Mathematics National Curriculum.

David Johnson is the Shell Professor of Mathematics Education. His research and development activities span the age range from upper primary school through A-level, with a focus on teaching and learning in school mathematics and the impact of Information Technology (IT). He was co-director of a DES national evaluation of the impact of IT on pupils' achievements in primary and secondary schools. Current research work is in the area of 'cognitive acceleration through/in school mathematics' in Years 7 and 8.

Alison Millett is a researcher in Mathematics Education with a special interest in primary school mathematics. Her background includes primary school teaching and management experience. Her current research activity is focused on primary teachers and teacher change in the planning and implementation of

Ma1, Using and Applying Mathematics, in a whole-school context. The work thus spans both the literature on teacher change and problem-solving in school mathematics.

Stephanie Prestage is a Lecturer in Mathematics Education, working mainly in the area of initial teacher training (secondary school mathematics). Her previous experience includes secondary school teaching in the Inner London Education Authority, ILEA, and participation in the Nuffield/ILEA/ULEAC/King's Graded Assessment in Mathematics, GAIM, project. She has also participated in development work related to Ma1 and numeracy.

PREFACE

In September 1993 a research team from King's College London, the University of Birmingham and the University of Cambridge Institute of Education completed a two-year research study to evaluate the implementation of the National Curriculum for mathematics at Key Stages 1, 2 and 3 (Askew *et al.*, 1993). The focus was on primary and secondary teachers and their perceptions and actions in a period of major change brought about by the move to a statutory national curriculum.

The book opens by tracing the evolution of the context from which the research was conceived. Drawing on official government documents and first-hand experience, a summary of events leading up to the publication of the first mathematics Order in 1989 precedes a highlighting of shifts in concerns, for both curriculum and assessment, over time; particular aspects in the dialogue and debate leading to the changes from the 1989 Order, through the subsequent Order in 1991 and up to the specification for the research, are included. This is followed by a summary of the research project in terms of its foci, methodology and data collection, selected findings and recommendations. Themes and issues arising from the work are identified, including those developed further in subsequent chapters.

Chapters 3–5 each takes a particular research focus and as such is complete in itself. The use made by teachers of commercial mathematics schemes, the professional development of teachers concerned with achieving 'ownership' of the curriculum, and perceptions of 'Using and Applying Mathematics' arising from teacher 'readings' of the National Curriculum documents are the three areas of focus.

The book closes with a consideration of the impact of the research on subsequent events. In particular, attention is given to the interplay of policy, politics and practice in the period 1993–94 – a period which included the Dearing review, the project team's input to this review and yet another 'new' mathematics Order (January 1995).

This book will be of interest not only to the research community but also to the teachers, educationists and policy-makers who have themselves been participants in this period of curriculum change. It gives a broad view of developing policy in the years leading up to the National Curriculum, with a closer focus, from those engaged in the evaluation of the implementation of the curriculum, on the intricacies of policy implementation and review – 'friction at the interface'.

ACKNOWLEDGEMENTS

Chapters 2–5 and the Appendices in this book include material already available in the two-volume report of the National Curriculum Council commissioned study published by the School Curriculum and Assessment Authority – see Askew *et al.*, 1993. For purposes of flow and presentation, the material amalgamated and reproduced from sections in the official report(s) has not been acknowledged as quotations. Justification for the inclusion of selected text is in terms of the now limited availability of the report and the need to provide a reasonably comprehensive 'picture' of the research methodology, Chapter 2, and the discussion in subsequent chapters.

GLOSSARY

Assessment/examination

APU	Assessment of Performance Unit
CATS	Consortium for Assessment and Testing in Schools
CSE	Certificate of Secondary Education
ENCA	Evaluation of National Curriculum Assessment
GCE	General Certificate of Education
GCSE	General Certificate of Secondary Education
SCAA	School Curriculum and Assessment Authority
SEAC	School Examinations and Assessment Council
SEC	Secondary Examinations Council
TGAT	Task Group on Assessment and Testing

Government agencies (national and local)

BTEC	Business and Technical Education Council
DES	Department of Education and Science
DfE	Department for Education
HMI	Her Majesty's Inspectorate
ILEA	Inner London Education Authority
LEA	Local education authority
NCET	National Council for Educational Technology
Ofsted	Office for Standards in Education
SCDC	School Curriculum Development Council
TTA	Teacher Training Agency

National Curriculum

AT(s)	Attainment target(s)
IT	Information technology

KS1	Key Stage 1 (Reception–Yr2, ages 5–7)
KS2	Key Stage 2 (Yr 3–6, ages 7–11)
KS3	Key Stage 3 (Yr 7–9, ages 11–14)
KS4	Key Stage 4 (Yr 10–11, ages 14–16)
Ma1	Mathematics attainment target 1 (1991) – 'Using and Applying Mathematics'
Ma2	Mathematics attainment target 2 (1991) – Number
Ma3	Mathematics attainment target 3 (1991) – Algebra
Ma4	Mathematics attainment target 4 (1991) – Shape and space
Ma5	Mathematics attainment target 5 (1991) – Handling data
NC	National Curriculum
NCC	National Curriculum Council
NSG	Non-statutory guidance
PC(s)	Profile Component(s) (1989)
PoS(s)	Programmes of study
SAT(s)	Standard Assessment Task(s)
SoA(s)	Statement(s) of attainment
UAM	'Using and Applying Mathematics'
Yr	Year

Professional associations

ASE	Association for Science Education
ATM	The Association of Teachers of Mathematics
MA	The Mathematical Association
NASUWT	National Association of Schoolmasters and Union of Women Teachers
NATE	National Association for the Teaching of English
NCTM	National Council of Teachers of Mathematics (US)
NUT	National Union of Teachers

Other

BCME	British Congress for Mathematics Education
BGC	Bishop Grosseteste College, Lincoln
BSRLM	British Society for Research on Learning in Mathematics
CATS	Consortium for Assessment and Testing in Schools
CMF	Children's Mathematical Frameworks Project
CSMS	Concepts in Secondary Mathematics and Science (research project)
ERA	Education Reform Act 1988
GAIM	Graded Assessment in Mathematics project
HE	Higher education
HoD	Head of department
Inset	Inservice education and training
ITT	Initial teacher training

LAMP	Low Attainers Mathematics Project
NFER	National Foundation for Educational Research
RAMP	Raising Attainment in Mathematics Project
SESM	Strategies and Errors in Secondary Mathematics Project
SMILE	Structured Mathematics Individualised Learning Experiment
SMP	School Mathematics Project (11–16)

THE CONTEXT OF THE RESEARCH – THE EVOLUTION OF THE NATIONAL CURRICULUM FOR MATHEMATICS

Margaret Brown
King's College London

INTRODUCTION

This chapter traces the development of a national curriculum in mathematics over the period from about 1975 to the start of the project Evaluation of the Implementation of National Curriculum Mathematics at Key Stages 1, 2 and 3 in September 1991.

The chapter is informed by the involvement of the author in developments throughout this period. Early on this was in marginal roles, as a member of the Schools Council Mathematics Committee, as a researcher consulted by the Cockcroft Committee and as director of a graded assessment project. The account becomes more personal as the roles became more central: as co-director of the national feasibility study in the primary phase, member of the National Curriculum Mathematics Working Group, director of a project producing non-statutory guidance, and grant-holder for the development of national tests at Key Stage (KS) 3.

It is sometimes thought that the National Curriculum (NC) was imposed on the English and Welsh education system in the Education Reform Act 1988 (ERA) like a bolt from the blue, with little prior warning. The haste of decision and implementation was indeed novel to the system. Nevertheless it is clear that from about the mid-1970s a gradual build-up towards a more centralised curriculum of some type had been taking place, following the traditional British process of consultation papers, committees and long-drawn-out discussions aimed at arriving at a consensus between all interested parties.

Throughout this process, mathematics has generally been the first subject to be tackled. Hence a study of the evolution of the NC in mathematics provides documentation not only of interest to those in mathematics education but also illuminates more general aspects of curriculum history.

The reasons for mathematics almost always being the first subject through the hoop seem likely to reflect three commonly held perceptions:

- The content of the mathematics curriculum is straightforward and un-controversial, since mathematics entails mainly knowledge of facts (e.g. multiplication tables) and procedures (e.g. long division, simultaneous equations).
- Since low standards of arithmetical performance are a constant problem, it is always politically popular to be seen to be taking some action.
- Since the teaching force in mathematics is weakly organised and relatively unpoliticised, there will be little opposition to enforcement of a centralised curriculum.

In retrospect, the last two of these perceptions have proved to be correct. While mathematical content has perhaps been rather more contentious than politicians have expected, the ideological disputes have been low key in comparison to those in, for example, English or history.

FIRST MOVES TOWARDS A CORE CURRICULUM: 1960–80

The Ruskin Speech

In fact the first expressed desire of a Minister of Education (Sir David Eccles) to 'unlock the secret garden' of the curriculum and become involved in curriculum specification was as far back as the early 1960s (Fowler, 1988), and resulted in the formation of a Curriculum Study Group within the Ministry, soon to become the Department of Education and Science (DES). However the transformation of this group into the union-dominated Schools Council enabled the ministerial intention to be quietly thwarted, especially under an incoming Labour government whose main concern was with the introduction of comprehensive education.

The next and more vigorous government statement of intention to venture into the curriculum area occurred 14 years later, contained in Prime Minister James Callaghan's 'Great Debate' Ruskin Speech in 1976. Evidence from employers of arithmetical shortcomings in industrial recruits was quoted as an important part of the justification for the need for higher standards.

The Assessment of Performance Unit

Again, the Callaghan intervention was not as sudden as it is sometimes presented to be. There had been a growing concern over the accountability of the education system in the early 1970s, following a series of black papers from the Right attacking educational standards (e.g. Cox and Dyson, 1969). One response had been a feasibility project into the national monitoring of mathematical standards, Tests of Attainment in Mathematics in Schools, based at the National Foundation for Educational Research (NFER) from 1972. This was a precursor to the creation in 1974 of the Assessment of Performance Unit (APU) at the DES with the aim of monitoring national standards and pinpointing sources of underachievement (Gipps and Goldstein, 1983).

Mathematics was not surprisingly the first subject to be surveyed, at both 11 and 15, annually, starting in 1978 (DES/APU, 1980a; 1980b). However the expenditure on this exercise proved hardly to be justified; standards were not spectacularly bad and little change was found over short time periods. Messages from the results were rarely simple or coherent, and even when they were, were neither effectively conveyed to nor acted upon by teachers. The light sampling methods and lack of public reporting of the results for a school gave teachers little incentive to try to cover the content tested in order to improve the rather diffuse notion of standards as measured by the tests. Thus an exercise that had the potential to define and dictate the mathematics curriculum was safely sidelined.

Nevertheless the continuing concerns expressed by mathematics educators at the restricted nature of the assessment instruments, and the eventually successful attempts to extend these more broadly into practical, problem-solving and group-work tasks, foreshadowed many later curriculum battles. The practical tests, and groups of trained testers in each area, formed a basis for many local education authority (LEA) assessments, both primary and secondary, developed during the early 1980s.

The involvement of LEAs

The major follow-up to the Ruskin Speech came from Shirley Williams, the Secretary of State for Education and Science in the Callaghan government, in the form of a green paper *Education in Schools: A Consultative Document* (DES, 1977a). The need for a 'core curriculum' was stated, if rather tentatively, and it was not clear whether it was a vague 'framework' or more precise specification which was intended. As one might expect from a Labour minister wary of upsetting teacher unions and LEAs, full roles were promised for all partners in the negotiation of such a core. LEAs, unions and professional associations, the Schools Council and other interests were to be consulted over the nature of a curriculum review, which each LEA would then be asked to conduct in partnership with its teachers.

The request, which was contained in Circular 14/77 (DES, 1977b), must have come as a surprise to LEAs, who had previously considered that responsibility for curriculum lay neither with them nor the DES, but at the level of the individual school, and indeed often *de facto* with the individual teacher. The Secretary of State had clearly adopted the tactic of avoiding the need for national legislation by using the LEAs to impose some degree of uniformity on their schools.

Her Majesty's Inspectorate initiatives at secondary level

Considering themselves to be the curriculum experts, and determined not to be outmanoeuvred by the DES, Her Majesty's Inspectorate (HMI) were simultaneously developing and publicising their own policy.

Initially, in a set of short papers on problems in mathematics, science and modern languages (HMI, 1977a), the notion of minimal goals in mathematics is discussed briefly and in rather negative terms. But by December 1977, HMI policy was clear and publication of a set of working papers, under the title *Curriculum 11–16* (DES, 1977c), argued strongly for a common curriculum in secondary education to 16. It rejected the option of defining a minimal core curriculum by issuing separate subject content lists, with particular emphasis on mathematics, English and science, which appeared to be favoured by the DES. Instead HMI proposed an entitlement for each pupil of eight areas of experience: aesthetic and creative, ethical, linguistic, mathematical, physical, scientific, social and political, and spiritual. In mathematics, as in other areas, a preliminary discussion of aims was followed by a set of basic content objectives (20 in mathematics).

HMI action in primary mathematics

A different set of 20 objectives was presented by HMI in a much more substantial monograph on primary mathematics, *Mathematics 5–11: A Handbook of Suggestions* (DES/HMI, 1979). Although in the HMI tradition this took a fairly enlightened view, including a broad curriculum and an emphasis on understanding, reasoning and communication, it included a long list of content which was more prescriptive than any previous HMI publication. HMI pronouncements have rarely had much direct audience in schools and this was no exception, although there was some immediate permeation via the large number of teachers registered in higher education (HE) institutions for the Primary Diploma of the Mathematical Association. In the longer term, mathematics textbooks and LEAs provided a mediating channel for translating the HMI programme into primary school practice.

The requirement for a curriculum review in each LEA contained in the 1977 green paper stimulated a process of meetings and consultations between many mathematics advisers and teachers aiming towards provision of local curriculum guidelines. In many LEAs primary mathematics was the first subject to be tackled. This may initially have reflected political pressure and uncertainties felt by teachers and headteachers about the content to be covered in the mathematics curriculum. Something of a vacuum had been left by the general abandonment of 11-plus examinations in the late 1960s and early 1970s, following the introduction of comprehensive non-selective secondary schools. The publication of the detailed HMI *Handbook* on primary mathematics is likely to have provided an additional stimulus.

Not all LEAs were equally active; indeed a final DES report (DES, 1979), before the change to a Conservative government, noted the general inadequacy of LEAs' information and policy regarding school curricula. Nevertheless by the time a pressing request for information on progress was issued to LEAs in 1983 (Circular 8/83), several of these primary mathematics guidelines were already implemented and in some cases were being extended to incorporate assessment systems, either formative or summative, for use during and/or at the end of primary education.

The period of office of Mark Carlisle, the first Secretary of State in the new Conservative government, saw further battles for curricular control between the DES and the HMI, with two DES papers (DES, 1980a; 1980b) against three from HMI – one of which showed HMI stealing a march on the DES by reporting results of implementation of the HMI version of the framework in 41 schools (DES/HMI, 1983). These publications continued and developed the two essentially different but equally centralist lines of argument, turning the screw a little further but containing little that was either new or particularly relevant to mathematics.

CURRICULUM CONVERGENCE – COCKCROFT AND THE GENERAL CERTIFICATE OF SECONDARY EDUCATION: 1981–84

The Cockcroft Committee

It was pressure not from DES or HMI but from a third group which finally produced national action in mathematics. The Parliamentary Expenditure Committee (1977) recommended among other things that an enquiry should be set up into the teaching of mathematics. They also expressed concern over both the unnecessary plethora of different examination syllabuses in mathematics and the dissatisfaction of employers about standards of numeracy, the latter repeating a theme of the Ruskin Speech. In 1978 the Secretary of State, Shirley Williams, set up a Committee of Inquiry into the Teaching of Mathematics in Schools, under the chairmanship of Sir Wilfred Cockcroft. In the event the committee was to complete most of its work after the change to a Conservative government in 1979.

The committee's investigations revealed surprisingly that industry and commerce were expressing little dissatisfaction with the mathematical skill levels of new entrants, perhaps because rising unemployment had enabled employers to be more selective in recruitment. The shortcomings were shown to be more in terms of a universally expressed lack of confidence in the subject, even among science graduates, and difficulty in applying knowledge or using it to communicate quantitatively.

The Cockcroft Foundation List

The Final Report (Cockcroft, 1982) was a model of consensus, and set recommendations which were widely accepted both in Britain and abroad. After much agonising it was decided to publish a Foundation List of basic mathematical competencies which almost all secondary pupils should be expected to achieve by the time they left school. Initial drafts involved bare statements of narrow context-free skills and procedures following the type of objectives which were then current in the Technician Education Council. (This group, which became BTEC – Business and Technical Education Council – later spread a more sophisticated version of this philosophy more widely into vocational education via the National Council for Vocational Qualifications.) However the Cockcroft Committee developed the initial draft of objectives into a final version in which they were expressed as understandings and processes as well as skills, and were to be applied within specific contexts. Even in this Foundation List the curriculum content was broad, avoiding a narrow concentration on number skills. Use of calculators and computers from an early age was also endorsed.

Thus the curriculum recommendations of the Cockcroft Committee continued strongly the spirit of earlier HMI reports, not surprisingly considering the fact that the secretary to the committee, entrusted with much of the drafting, was a leading HMI.

Other Cockcroft recommendations

Clear recommendations were given that the way to increase confidence and application skills was to broaden methods of teaching and assessment to include practical work, problem-solving, investigation and discussion, alongside the traditional exposition and practice. New evidence on the wide range of attainment at all ages, from the APU and the mathematics component of the Concepts in Secondary Mathematics and Science Project (CSMS) (Hart, 1981), also prompted a call for greater differentiation in both syllabus and examinations.

Thus the Cockcroft Committee established two important features in the early 1980s: that of breadth and utilitarian applicability of curriculum, and that of differentiation. Both of these were to influence other subjects, not least because of the alliance formed between the Committee Chairman and Sir Keith Joseph, who became the Secretary of State in the final stages of the committee. The appointment of Sir Wilfred Cockcroft to chair the newly created Secondary Examinations Council (SEC) provided an official channel for this influence, but the voice of both Sir Wilfred and Sheila Browne, Her Majesty's Chief Inspector of Schools, can also be perceived in many of the more benign effects of the Joseph era.

The implementation of the Cockcroft proposals

The implementation of the Cockcroft Report took place through four main routes:

- New curriculum schemes embodying many of the recommendations – in particular the new School Mathematics Project materials at secondary level (SMP 11–16) which were used ultimately in more than 70 per cent of schools.
- DES-funded advisory teachers ('Cockcroft missionaries'), both primary and secondary, appointed in each LEA to spread their own good practice by working mainly in classrooms alongside other teachers.
- Curriculum and graded assessment schemes for the lowest attainers in the 14–16 age group based on the Foundation List and broader teaching modes, in particular the Low Attainers in Mathematics Project (LAMP), and later the Raising Attainment in Mathematics Project (RAMP) at the West Sussex Institute of Higher Education, the SMP Graduated Assessment Scheme and various LEA schemes, including especially the Nuffield/ Inner London Education Authority/King's College Graded Assessment in Mathematics (GAIM).
- The new General Certificate in Secondary Education (GCSE).

The relative effectiveness of these channels would make an interesting study, but there is no doubt that taken together they exerted an enormous influence at secondary level.

The GCSE examination system

The most powerful engine for curriculum change was probably the introduction of the new GCSE examination system, designed initially to cater for the top 60 per cent of pupils. There had previously been two separate examination systems, the General Certificate in Education (GCE) O-level for the top 20 per cent, and the Certificate of Secondary Education (CSE) for the next 40 per cent. However approximately 85 per cent of the age group are now entered for mathematics at GCSE.

The discussions about the introduction of a common examination had been going on within the Schools Council since the mid-1960s, driven by the needs of the growing number of comprehensive schools. Successful trials took place in the 1970s, but a final decision was held up by Shirley Williams' convening of a further enquiry (the Waddell Committee).

It was therefore left to the first Conservative Secretary of State, Mark Carlisle, to pick up from the Labour government the drive towards greater curriculum standardisation and to propose that any such new examination should be the vehicle for greater uniformity of curriculum, via the route of establishing 'national criteria' in each major subject. These would need to be satisfied by all examination board syllabuses which bore specific subject titles.

National criteria for GCSE

Before any firm commitment was to be made to a common examination, subject groups were set up by the DES to draft specimen criteria. However there was considerable dissatisfaction that these groups were mainly drawn from the ranks of the private examination boards, side-stepping the Schools Council which still had official responsibility for curriculum and examinations until its closure in 1984. Thus what was to be in effect the first draft of a national curriculum was entrusted to neither teachers, HMI nor curriculum experts. This was the first of many occasions on which the Conservative distrust of 'the educational establishment' was manifested.

After further delay the final go-ahead for the new GCSE was announced by the new Secretary of State, Sir Keith Joseph, in mid 1984. Allowing a period for finalising the national criteria and then syllabus and examination development by the examination boards, 1988 was agreed for the first examinations. All arrangements were to be under the new Cockcroft-chaired SEC, which had been established in 1984 as part of the replacement for the discredited Schools Council. Greater centralism was signalled by the decision of the Secretary of State personally to nominate the members of the SEC and its lesser partner the School Curriculum Development Council (SCDC).

The job of drawing up draft and later final national criteria had been much eased in mathematics by the work of the Cockcroft Committee. In contrast to some other subjects in which criteria took the form only of general requirements relating to processes to be assessed, in mathematics the criteria went further and specified more detailed common content lists for the different levels of award. As proposed by the Cockcroft Committee, an overlapping series of stepped papers was the preferred model. The syllabus for the foundation level (List 1) was almost a direct copy of the Cockcroft Foundation List.

Thus in mathematics the consensus achieved by the Cockcroft Report helped to avoid the type of controversy caused in such subjects as science and history by the personal intervention of the Secretary of State at a late stage.

The general criteria for the new GCSE required a proportion of the marks in all subjects to be allocated to teacher-marked coursework, from a minimum of *20 per cent* to a maximum of 100 per cent. This reflected a tradition in many subjects of mode-3 (school-based) examinations in the previous CSE, and a limited number of coursework-based examinations, mainly in English, in the higher-status GCE O-level.

In mathematics the coursework requirement also reflected the Cockcroft-specified need for examination of practical, oral, problem-solving and investigational elements, including use of calculators and computers, which could not be assessed by more traditional means. Nevertheless in mathematics at least 50 per cent of the marks were normally expected to be awarded by written examination and teachers were uniquely granted a three-year delay period, until 1991, before a coursework element became compulsory. This allowed more than 90 per cent of teachers to put off its introduction for at least a year, and most to delay longer, introducing only the minimum percentage in 1991. Ironically by then the tide had turned against mathematics coursework, and by the time of the first NC-based GCSE in 1994 it was again possible to avoid it.

Graded tests for low attainers

A recommendation in the Cockcroft Report referred to the introduction of graded tests for low-attaining pupils in the lowest 40 per cent who were then considered to be below the entry standard for CSE or any new common examination system. This recommendation coincided with one of the beliefs underlying Sir Keith Joseph's educational policies, that this group should have a vocational and non-academic programme separate from that for other pupils.

Graded tests were first introduced into English schools in modern languages, and were based on the functional approaches used in the system of examinations for interpreters, as well as drawing on experience in testing leisure-related skills such as athletics, swimming and music. They were introduced to provide motivation in the form of regular recognition of attainment, especially for pupils in the early years of the new comprehensive schools, many of whom expected to give up their study of modern languages by the age of 14 and were therefore reluctant to engage. The graded tests were an immediate success with pupils, teachers and parents, and significantly boosted the numbers electing to continue with their study of modern languages (Harrison, 1982).

As a result of the Cockcroft recommendations two graded test projects relating to secondary low attainers were funded by the DES in 1983. One of these, based at the NFER, was to investigate feasibility issues and to gather information about the many LEA tests for low attainers then under development; several of these had incorporated ideas from the practical tests for 15-year-olds developed by the APU.

The second project was in co-ordination with the newly developed SMP 11–16 project. This major post-Cockcroft curriculum development project profited from the membership on the Cockcroft Committee of the Executive Director, John Hersee, and, like the Cockcroft Report, drew on the results of the recently published CSMS research (Hart, 1981). The materials were based on a utilitarian philosophy and were well matched to the mathematical level of most mainstream pupils, with the result that more than two-thirds of second-ary schools adopted the scheme. To enable differentiation in mixed-ability groups in the lower secondary school, short booklets were introduced, and used mainly in an individualised fashion. Although setting in later years was catered for by different tiers of textbooks, some schools carried on working in an individualised way, especially in the lower groups. Following the Cockcroft proposals a graduated assessment scheme for low attainers was already well advanced; the DES money helped to extend the scheme and to evaluate it.

Investigations and problem-solving

Thus the situation in secondary schools by the mid-1980s was that, thanks to the widespread adoption of SMP 11–16 and similar schemes, there was to a great extent a common content curriculum in mathematics based on the Cock-croft proposals, supplemented by the national GCSE criteria.

Schools were however considerably slower to introduce broader teaching methods. A strong influence was the LAMP project, led by Afzal Ahmed, a Cockcroft Committee member, at West Sussex Institute of Higher Education, funded by the DES to run alongside the two graded test projects. LAMP, and its successor, RAMP, emphasised success for pupils through investigative work and used local networks of teachers to build up a bank of experience and ideas to give considerable support for other teachers (West Sussex Institute, 1987). Part of this support was via a new Mathematical Association Diploma for Teachers of Low Attainers, similar in nature to that of the primary diploma.

The West Sussex approach to investigatory work as a way of learning con-tent as well as process was echoed by many of the new LEA advisory teachers, appointed as a result of the Cockcroft recommendations. These teachers were expected to spread their expertise by working in classrooms alongside other teachers, an approach which appeared to be successful.

However the majority of secondary teachers were mainly stimulated to in-troduce new teaching methods by the threat of compulsory introduction of 20 per cent coursework by 1991. Several examination boards translated the coursework tasks into rather predictable, highly structured 'investigations', while keeping their content papers fairly traditional in form. This meant that many schools introduced occasional 'investigation lessons', with the bulk of the work for these tasks often done at home, alongside standard class teaching or individualised teaching.

In the primary sector, there had been progress in many LEAs on guidelines, based first on the HMI objectives (DES/HMI, 1979), and later by the Cockcroft recommendations. Many schools had adopted new curriculum schemes such as Scottish Primary Mathematics and Nuffield 5–11, which broadly followed the HMI content. This move to new schemes may have militated against the introduction of more practical and investigational work encouraged in the Cockcroft Report. Certainly the efforts of primary advisory teachers appointed to implement these changes, following up valiant attempts since the mid-1960s by HMIs such as Edith Biggs (Schools Council, 1965), and supplemented by the graduation of cohorts of teachers from Mathematical Association Diploma courses, seemed to have produced little evidence of change in the classroom styles of most primary teachers.

OBJECTIVES AND TARGETS – THE BUILD-UP TO THE NC: 1985–86

Criterion-referenced assessment

Sir Keith Joseph found attractive one particular aspect of graded tests: that levels were described in terms of particular skills which formed the basis of the assessment. Thus attainment of a level could convey information to employers and further education about what competencies new recruits possessed, as well as producing clarity of aims for pupils and teachers.

Considerable work on criterion-referencing had been undertaken in the USA (e.g. Popham, 1969), but this was mainly in a narrow behaviourist mode with multiple-choice testing. More relevant developments in this area were being undertaken in Scotland as part of the introduction of a new standard-grade examination scheme (Brown, 1980). A similar move towards assessment of competencies was fostered by BTEC and was the basis of the introduction of profile statements and college-based assessment of objectives in the further education sector in England.

At secondary level, movements in this direction were pioneered by LEAs led by three outstanding chief education officers who regularly conferred: Bill (later Sir William) Stubbs of the Inner London Education Authority (ILEA), Gordon Hainsworth of Manchester and Tim Brighouse of Oxfordshire. Frustrated by the delays in introducing a common examination and concerned at low standards of attainment resulting from low motivation in comprehensive schools, they each combined with local examination boards to explore alternative assessment frameworks linked in with pastorally based Records of Achievement. The Northern Examination and Assessment Board produced a modular system of units and credits, the Oxford Certificate of Educational Achievement went for profiling statements, and the London Group explored both modular systems and graded assessment. Graded assessment was a step forward from the graded test movement in incorporating ongoing teacher assessment in preference to end-of-year tests.

Graded assessment

GAIM was part of the London Group involving the ILEA, London-based examination boards and King's College. When GAIM was refused funding by the DES as part of the post-Cockcroft initiatives on the basis that the scheme covered the whole attainment range, not only low attainers, the Nuffield Foundation agreed to step in to provide support.

GAIM developed a set of 15 levels defined by means of conceptually based criteria in each of six topic areas (logic, number, algebra, measures, space and statistics). Criteria were partly based on research results, including the earlier CSMS research (Hart, 1981) which was carried out at Chelsea (later to become part of King's College London). The ILEA SMILE scheme and the expert knowledge of a large group of teachers assisted in the initial formulation and placing of criteria, which were later refined by trialling.

Each GAIM level was designed to constitute roughly one year's work, with the top seven levels equivalent to the grades in the new GCSE so as to enable the scheme to be used as the basis for GCSE awards. (After considerable battles, grades D–G were awarded starting in 1989 on 100 per cent coursework, following a waiver of the national criteria for mathematics, and in the following year grades A–C were also awarded on the basis of coursework in addition to a school-marked validation test.)

The main vehicle for the assessments was a centrally provided bank of investigations and problem-solving tasks which each crossed many levels and many topics, together with ongoing teacher assessment using tests and/or other classroom work (Brown, 1992a). Pupils had access to the criteria and were expected to provide evidence of their own attainment and keep their own records, and moderation was carried out by assessors who visited clusters of schools to audit the records. The scheme was constantly trialled and improved over six years with the number of trial schools growing from 10 to over 70.

Grade criteria for GCSE

Soon after he took over as Secretary of State for Education and Science, Sir Keith Joseph suggested that the national criteria then being developed for GCSE should be amended to provide criteria for attainment of particular grades. He was told that work on the criteria was almost complete and that a change of direction would hold up the introduction of the courses in 1986 for first examination in 1988. As a compromise it was agreed that the initial version of the national criteria would include a broad but not prescriptive description of competencies at grades A, C and F, but that under the new SEC a programme of development of grade criteria would be undertaken to be implemented at a later stage.

In fact the grade criteria exercise was undertaken (SEC, 1985a; 1985b) but the attempt turned out to be something of a débâcle, and implementation was abandoned. There were considerable differences between subjects, with mathematics listing too many detailed criteria to be feasibly examined in a short examination, and English listing criteria which were so few and vague that they could not be used to distinguish between different grades. The GCSE examination groups were less than enthusiastic, as a successful result would have required major changes in examining techniques. It would also have undermined their existing expertise which combined statistical norm-referenced approaches with an almost mystical form of criterion-referencing which depended on the tacit judgement of chief examiners.

The white paper *Better Schools*

The intention to embark upon grade criteria was referred to in the white paper of 1985 *Better Schools* (DES/WO, 1985), as part of a more widespread embracing of objectives in education leading to broad criterion-referencing of examinations and assessment. The white paper, which was heralded in Sir Keith Joseph's North of England Speech of 1984, was remarkable in forming a watershed between the years of consensus in education and the embattled years which followed. The document itself was, like the Cockcroft Report, a model of clarity and coherence. It succeeded in drawing together the various strands of educational development since 1976, integrating the HMI and the DES views, and presenting the future directions. It started from a concise statement of the problem:

> . . . the Government believes that, not least in the light of what is being achieved in other countries, the standards now generally attained by our pupils are neither as good as they can be, nor as good as they need to be if young people are to be equipped for the world of the twenty-first century. By the time they leave school, pupils need to have acquired, far more than at present, the qualities and skills required for work in a technological age.
>
> (DES/WO, 1985, sec. 9)

This was followed by a listing of the aims of education repeated from earlier papers (e.g. DES, 1977a), which was so imbued with liberal spirit that it now appears redolent of another era. For example the first aim listed was '(1) to enable pupils to develop lively, inquiring minds, the ability to question and argue rationally and to apply themselves to tasks, and physical skills' (DES/WO, 1985, sec. 44). The requirement for a curriculum which was broad, balanced, relevant and differentiated was carefully argued in the following paragraph.

This white paper proceeded to introduce in paragraphs 80 and 81, for the first time, the notion of attainment targets for the end of the primary phase, to parallel grade criteria for GCSE in the secondary phase. The difficulties of specifying attainment targets were noted, with reference to the particular problem of dealing with a broad attainment range. This led on, in paragraphs 82 and 83, to the need for continuous teacher assessment to monitor achievement of these targets in order to plan the curriculum, inform pupils and parents of progress, and for the school to evaluate its own performance. Finally the need for formal certification of pupils by public examinations was accepted, but even here it was qualified by the phrase 'to which teacher assessment of course work contributes substantially' (para 84, p. 27).

Better Schools was the first public document to establish an intention to set centrally determined attainment targets for the end of primary education, but stops well short of any requirement for a full national curriculum or programme of study. Indeed Lord Joseph, as he later became, spoke passionately against the imposition of the national curriculum when the bill leading to the 1988 Act came before the House of Lords.

It seemed likely that the shift of emphasis from secondary to primary education was partly caused by growing public concern about those primary schools which were abusing their freedom to determine their own curricula. This stemmed from media attention given to the notorious case of William Tyndale Junior School in inner London in the late 1970s, in which it was suggested that little attention was given to any teaching of basic numeracy and literacy skills, or indeed any form of traditional knowledge.

There had been surprisingly little fuss about the introduction of what was in effect, at least in the more rigidly controlled subjects such as mathematics, a nationally imposed syllabus for secondary education specified by the national criteria for GCSE. With the exception of minor skirmishes over the Secretary of State's personal intervention in subjects such as history and science, the national criteria were accepted as part of the GCSE package for which teachers had been waiting so long. Encouraged by this relative lack of opposition, Sir Keith Joseph was intent on extending control to the primary phase using similar means.

Again there was some concern expressed by the educational establishment over growing centralism, but little clear opposition from classroom teachers.

Curriculum objectives from HMI

Alongside the white paper, the HMI were continuing with their detailed publication of curriculum objectives under the title *Curriculum Matters*, this time apparently with the blessing of the DES. There was a break in tradition in 1984 when English rather than mathematics was the first subject to be tackled (DES/HMI, 1984). The publication was premature, especially with respect to the more general announcements by the DES and HMI, and was greeted by an angry response among English teachers at being unexpectedly presented with a reductionist list of objectives for ages 11 and 16.

A more general treatment of the whole curriculum was second in the HMI series (DES/HMI, 1985). It developed the 'areas of experience' approach of earlier HMI publications (HMI, 1977b), but added to it a problematic dissection of the curriculum into 'knowledge', 'concepts', 'skills' and 'attitudes'.

The mathematics' document *Mathematics from 5 to 16* (DES, 1985) quickly followed this. It was firmly based on the Cockcroft proposals, although with more attempt at explication of general mathematical strategies (such as 'trial-and-error methods', 'proving and disproving'), good work habits and attitudes. In spite of a heavy weighting on 'knowledge', it had a much easier ride than the English publication. Nevertheless there was some criticism of both the general notion and the detail of the lists of objectives 'for most pupils at the age of 11' and the equivalent for age 16.

Feasibility study on attainment targets and assessment for age 11

This relatively muted response to what was in effect a draft set of national attainment targets for ages 11 and 16 encouraged the DES to select mathematics as the first subject in which to develop operational attainment targets and assessment in mathematics for age 11. Around Easter 1986, bids were invited to undertake a one-year feasibility study; the aim was on a basis of examination of current practice to formulate a proposal for a three- to four-year research and development project to arrive at a national set of attainment targets and a related assessment, trialled and ready to implement.

The briefing document itself was an interesting juxtaposition of DES-style and HMI-style prose, linking the DES need for reliable summative information for the purpose of monitoring standards to the HMI-backed importance of formative and diagnostic assessment in order to improve standards in the classroom. These purposes and, as a result, the two agencies which supported them, have been in continuous tension during the development and implementation of national assessment.

The contract was won by a team based at King's College London, in recognition of expertise in both exploring and assessing the development of numeracy among junior-age pupils (Denvir and Brown, 1986) and in developing and implementing graded assessment in the GAIM project (Brown, 1992a).

The project's enquiries among LEAs which had well developed primary mathematics guidelines and were in the course of implementing assessment schemes at or around age 11 revealed a number of interesting and contrasting models, including traditional standardised pencil-and-paper tests, graded tests, practical and one-to-one tests, and profiling schemes. Following trialling in one area of number, a mathematics framework was proposed for the whole primary age group, with attainment targets (corresponding to the later 'statements of attainment') arranged into local hierarchies which could be grouped into broad levels within three topics: logical reasoning, number and measure (weighted as double) and space (Denvir, Brown and Eve, 1987).

Various forms of assessment were trialled and the establishment of a national item bank was recommended. Teachers would draw on these items to standardise their own assessment, with moderation through local teacher groups and inspectors. An eight-year programme of teacher professional development was outlined which would include thorough consultation, development and piloting of targets and assessments, to be followed by a programme of teacher development. This would have enabled a fully prepared teaching force to start national implementation of the teaching and assessing of the first area of mathematics in September 1992, with the final topic in 1995 (ironically the same date as the third amended version of the mathematics NC was completed). However, while this feasibility study was taking place from September 1986 to 1987, the pace of movement towards a national curriculum was accelerating.

THE FIRST VERSION OF THE NC: 1986–89

Announcement of a NC

Almost immediately after the start of the feasibility study, Sir Keith Joseph resigned as Secretary of State, and his place was taken by Kenneth Baker. Baker was clearly impatient of the slow pace of progress envisaged, and was determined to have a more rapid implementation.

He was also influenced by a report from the radical Right (Prais and Wagner, 1985), which appeared to show that one of the reasons for the UK's poor industrial performance compared to that of Germany was low mathematical standards. In fact the evidence cited was weak and the argument tenuous, but it was used by Prais and his colleagues, including fellow economist Professor Brian Griffiths in the Prime Minister's Central Policy Unit, to push the need for a firmly specified national curriculum in mathematics. Prais' view was that this should be of a traditional nature focusing on number skills and laying down the content and teaching method to be used in each year – thus going well beyond the Joseph notion of a set of attainment targets for ages 11 and 16. (Interestingly, as the mathematics feasibility study report documented, Germany had no national curriculum, and the curriculum for each region (*Land*) was little more prescriptive than the UK's LEA guidelines. In all but one of the regions, there were no external tests and no agreed assessment criteria; grades in mathematics were subjective, teacher based and unpublished.)

Baker was also impressed by Donald Naismith, the Chief Education Officer for Croydon LEA in Greater London. In Croydon, success had been achieved in specifying mathematics targets together with associated testing at 7, 9, 11 and 14, with the results forming the basis of comparisons between schools.

In January 1987 the Secretary of State made a speech announcing his intention to implement a national curriculum in order to impose control upon the currently 'maverick' provision and thus raise standards to meet those of the UK's competitors. By April, spurred on no doubt by the prospect of an imminent general election, he announced that there would be attainment targets, programmes of study and national assessment at ages 7, 9, 11, 14 and 16 (in May's election manifesto age 9 disappeared). The programmes of study were a newly introduced notion following the Prais notion of curriculum specification, and were defined rather vaguely as 'what was to be taught'. Working groups in each subject would be appointed to draft the attainment targets, programmes of study and subject assessment guidelines; a further group would be formed to draw up the general assessment arrangements. In July, after the election in June, a hurriedly put together consultation document *The National Curriculum 5–16* was issued.

All this was happening in the full knowledge that the mathematics feasibility study for age 11, not due to report until the end of September, would recommend a much longer-term programme of consultation, development and trialling. In the event the outcome of the study was not made public until late November 1986, and only after the report had been leaked to the press.

Teachers' unions and the professional associations complained bitterly about the requirement for responses by the end of September, which made full consultation difficult. The Education Reform Bill (of which the NC was a minor part) was in print by November, with little notice having been taken of the responses (Haviland, 1988); after many parliamentary battles, the Education Reform Act (ERA) received Royal Assent in July 1988.

The Mathematics Working Group: early problems

The first brief meetings of newly appointed Working Groups in Mathematics and Science took place in July 1987, ahead of the consultation period, and the groups were given until the following May to produce recommendations. Meanwhile the Task Group on Assessment and Testing (TGAT) had only until the end of December 1987 to come up with a common framework and assessment arrangements (DES/WO, 1987).

The Mathematics Working Group started in earnest in September. Although the group was fairly representative in composition, it was chaired by a professor of physics, Roger Blin-Stoyle, and the secretary was a science HMI drafted into the DES. This sign of distrust in the mathematical establishment was in contrast to the science group which was chaired by a professor of science education, Jeff Thompson, and the assessment group, TGAT, which was chaired by a professor of science education with expertise in educational assessment, Paul Black.

Although it had been the Secretary of State's intention to remove the influence of HMI, the eventual presence on the committee of the Staff HMI for mathematics, Jim Mayhew, who was able to clear other work and involve colleagues where necessary, with the full-time HMI secretary as ally, meant that HMI had considerable control over the end-product. HMI were thus at least partially victorious in their long-running battle with the DES. Nevertheless the victory was no more than partial. The HMI strategy was to devote much initial energy to the agreement of general aims, preferably those put forward by the HMI, and to emphasise personal qualities and attitudes, communication and problem-solving strategies. In the latter he was backed up by the industrialist on the group, Ray Peacock. This agenda was in conflict with the continuing concentration on content favoured by the DES, following the lead of the minister. In the final outcome the HMI aspects were for a variety of reasons to be much reduced in scope.

The HMI line was strongly opposed by Professor Sig Prais who let it be known that he had a direct line to the Prime Minister, Margaret Thatcher. Prais was impatient to move swiftly to specifying a list of fixed attainment targets for different ages in terms of traditional arithmetical skills, such as adding fractions and knowing multiplication tables.

The university educationists, in particular Hugh Burkhardt and Hilary Shuard, took a different view again, being keen to produce a curriculum which was broad and took fully into account recent international developments in curricula, relating in particular to both contemporary mathematics and the use of calculators and computers. The educationists also were thought by some to be initially indulging in needlessly academic arguments, both with each other and over the nature of the exercise, trying to resolve what was meant in the brief by a programme of study or by attainment targets suitable for below-average, average and above-average pupils at the end of each key stage. It became clear that the legislation was, like Baker's poll tax, being pushed through in a 'gung-ho' fashion with little thinking-through having taken place either of the details of implementation or of the consequences. DES officials could not cast any light on what was required, pointing out that this was the role of the group. Interestingly, although the report of the feasibility study was circulated, it was not discussed by the group at any point.

In the event some of the educationists led the group into rejecting the age-orientated brief and the allied subcommittee structure proposed. It was felt that a separate specification of targets for below-average, average and above-average groups of pupils at 7, 11, 14 and 16 would be inequitable as it would lead to early and fixed labelling of pupils into one of these three categories. However single sets of age-based targets would inevitably result in lower-attaining pupils being branded as failures and insufficient challenge for faster-learning pupils.

Fears were expressed that separate subcommittees for each age group, each with their own agendas, would lead to a discontinuous curriculum. This would be particularly unfortunate as it was pointed out that research results showed that some low attainers at 14, for example, were mathematically less advanced than average pupils at age 11.

Hence the working group decided, to the consternation of the Chairman and DES representative, to start by specifying progression of skills and activities within each of several strands of process and content. Thus in order technically to conform to the Secretary of State's requirements, the original notion of an attainment target as a specific skill to be achieved by a particular age, already stretched in the brief to allow for pupils at different levels of attainment at that age, had to be reinterpreted to include levels of attainment across different ages. This reinterpretation was undertaken in the knowledge that similar arguments replacing ages with levels as the basis for the national assessment framework, using evidence from graded assessment projects which used such a system, were going on within TGAT.

The Chairman had been somewhat shocked at the first meeting when the majority of the group confessed that they were either opposed to, or at best very concerned about the effects of, a national curriculum. Graham (1993) reported that the Secretary of State accused the members of being subversive of the government's intentions; this was true to the extent that most felt that they were engaged in a damage limitation exercise. They recognised that a national curriculum was inevitable, and their main aim was to maintain a broad curriculum in the spirit of Cockcroft, in particular to prevent the Prais agenda of a narrow list of arithmetical procedures. Nevertheless it would be true to say that most members did see some positive advantages in being able to implement certain desirable features on a national scale.

Thus a variety of different philosophies and agendas (Ernest, 1991) was represented among group members. Not surprisingly the determination of many of the group not to compromise led to fierce battles, even over the minutes of meetings, and resulted in slow progress. The Chairman and Professor Prais resigned in November 1987, and the interim report (DES, 1987) was justifiably criticised by the Secretary of State as being inadequate (Graham, 1993). Although considerable groundwork had been done by the group, little other than rather vague general aims was in a form appropriate for publication. Moreover progress was held up considerably by the requirement, only three months into the task, of having to negotiate within a warring committee an agreed interim report for national consultation.

The Mathematics Working Group: further issues

The next Chairman was Duncan Graham, again a non-mathematician, who up till then had taken a 'lay' role and had remained on the edge of the group, having missed several meetings. He was however an experienced operator as the Chief Executive for Humberside and an ex-chief education officer, and was determined to knock heads together if necessary in order to meet the May deadline. At his insistence, new members were added, argumentative members were given little scope to cause distractions, some problematic issues were determinedly side-stepped, and progress was made.

The new TGAT framework of ten progressive levels, each not limited to a particular age but defined in relation to median performance at a specific age, was generally welcomed. Not surprisingly given the communication between members of the groups, the levels and the proposed TGAT continuous attainment target strands, gathered into profile components (PCs) for reporting purposes, fitted with the ways of working within the Mathematics Group.

The content organisation was simplified by reducing to 15 the originally envisaged total of 25 or so attainment targets, but with the sad loss of an important area of 'discrete mathematics', which the Chairman considered to be too esoteric, even when reformulated under the title 'applied logic'. The attainment targets were as follows:

- Number: Number and number notation
                             Number operations
                             Estimation and approximation
- Number/algebra: Patterns and generalisations
- Algebra: Functions, formulae and equations
                             Graphical representation
- Measurement: Estimation and measurement
- Shape and space: Properties of shapes
                             Location and transformation
- Handling data: Collect, record and process data
                             Represent and interpret data
                             Estimate and calculate probabilities
- Practical applications: Using mathematics
                             Communication skills
                             Personal qualities

Thus the working group felt broadly satisfied that they had maintained the spirit of the Cockcroft Report, maintaining a broad curriculum and a flavour of practical work/problem-solving/investigation.

Two major ongoing and linked problems over the content were methods of computation and the place of information technology (IT). Most of the group were strongly committed to a clearer emphasis on mental arithmetic and the use of calculators in primary schools; nevertheless there was clear ministerial pressure to maintain skills in pencil-and-paper arithmetic. An eleventh-hour compromise was reached in the latter by agreeing some competencies which had to be achieved without a calculator, but without specifying any formal method (such as 'long multiplication').

Although there were many who favoured increasing emphasis on the use of computers in mathematics, the group decided reluctantly that teachers would have enough problems with the introduction of the NC and new areas such as 'handling data'. The group were also aware that there would be no time to issue new teaching materials before the implementation date in 1989. Hence there was in the attainment targets very little compulsory requirement for use of computers, although they figured more extensively in the programmes of study.

There was no further concern over the number of the attainment targets since the TGAT recommendation that they should be grouped into profile components for assessment and reporting purposes was accepted. (TGAT had indeed made the recommendation of not more than three or four profile components on seeing that both science and mathematics groups were heading for larger numbers of attainment targets than it was sensible to report separately.) However there was a problem over how to group the targets into profile components. The six topic areas gave too many; the Chairman and Secretary of State favoured three: knowledge, skills and applications. The group rejected the split between knowledge and skills. A reluctant compromise was reached of retaining applications separate while splitting the content targets in two, each containing knowledge, skills and understanding in a range of topics. Because of the dominance of number and measures over algebra in the primary school and the reversal of this in the later stages of the secondary school, it was decided to group these areas together to maintain an approximately equal weighting between the two. The profile components (PCs) thus became

1. knowledge, skills and understanding in number, algebra and measures;
2. knowledge, skills and understanding in shape and space and handling data; and
3. practical applications of mathematics.

Each attainment target contained statements of attainment at each of ten levels, two years apart; for example, Level 2 statements comprised those competencies which could be expected of the average 7-year-old, Level 6 those of the average 15-year-old, and Level 9 those corresponding to an A-grade at GCSE. Although the GCSE national criteria and the GAIM project provided some guidance in identifying statements and placing them at different levels, there were a number of problems. In particular it proved impossible to level the targets in PC3. In some cases, such as 'personal qualities', this was because it was difficult to identify any hierarchy of progression. In 'communication skills' the difficulty level clearly depended on the content as much as on the mode of communication. Although there might have been some progression in 'using mathematics' (problem-solving strategies), there was insufficient work done to identify it. Hence the attainment targets in PC3 were levelled at each age rather than in 10 progressive levels. The group recognised that this was something of a hostage to fortune, but were keen to keep these areas and, given the enormous time pressure, there seemed little else that could be done.

The second problem concerned the level at which to place some of the statements. In some cases, placing them at a level where research showed that the majority of pupils could master them made it appear that the expectations were low, for example that the average pupil would not reach a reasonable understanding of decimals until well into the secondary school. The group decided therefore to move many of the statements down a level or two so as to appear to have confidence that standards would be raised to what was perceived to be an acceptable level. However several members were concerned that the first test results would then be likely to demonstrate that pupils were not meeting expectations. This decision had a further consequence in that it left empty much of the later levels, especially Levels 9 and 10. These had to be filled hastily and somewhat arbitrarily without proper consideration or debate.

One feature on which the group were insistent, and which was later to remain very popular among teachers, was that the statements of attainment within the levels were all illustrated by examples, in order to make clearer the meaning of the statements, and the level of difficulty intended.

Finally the group had had problems over the formulation of a programme of study. They felt that having specified the attainment targets in great detail, and drawn attention to the range and distribution of expected levels at the end of each key stage, there was nothing much left to say except to indicate important general principles about the variety of teaching activities which should be provided. Some additional principles were also added for each key stage. After the group had agreed the report there was an indication that this material was not suitable for inclusion in statutory orders, so the secretary and DES officials decided that the only solution was also to insert a summary of the attainment targets denoted as a 'map' of the curriculum.

A section on assessment expressed the view of the group that the national standard assessment tasks should exemplify good classroom practice and be varied in length, including long problem-solving items as well as short tests. The national assessment should, as TGAT recommended, be there only to sample attainment within each profile component so as to moderate results of teacher assessment. There was never any suggestion that within national tests each attainment target should be assessed and reported separately.

The working group put in many additional hours in order to complete the exercise on time. There were a number of last-minute compromises over the wording of the prose passages – the group mainly but not universally giving in to the Chairman's advice over what was politically acceptable. (For example the language of 'problem-solving' and 'investigations' were replaced by 'practical applications', and the multicultural piece supplied by the DES was reluctantly incorporated.) Nevertheless the group were generally satisfied that they had produced a workable and acceptable scheme, although they were very concerned that there had not been time within about eight months of occasional meetings to get all the details right.

Later amendments to the working group report

The Chairman, who had by now been appointed as Chairman and Chief Executive of the new National Curriculum Council (NCC), had pulled off a considerable feat, through continual negotiation of the limits of what was acceptable between the Secretary of State and the group. The final product was thus greeted with considerable relief both by Kenneth Baker and by the teaching profession.

However it was known that there was continuing ministerial concern about PC3, in particular that it was vague and unassessable, and did not conform to the levels model. The Chairman, anticipating problems, asked HMI to try to come up with a properly levelled and tougher set of targets by the end of the consultation period.

The report had been published in the middle of the summer holidays in August 1988, once again angering teachers' organisations and LEAs, who had first to co-ordinate school responses by the requirement to respond by early autumn. The large response was generally welcoming, with more than 80 per cent supporting the existence of the separate PC3, 'Practical Applications of Mathematics'. Nevertheless the NCC, who were running the consultation, decided that a compromise was necessary. The content had been revised by HMI with advice from some of the other group members so as to relevel and stiffen the attainment targets on 'Communication skills' and 'Using mathematics' (i.e. problem-solving skills). The problematic attainment target 'Personal qualities' was replaced by elements of what later became 'Reasoning, logic and proof', largely salvaged from the 'applied logic' target previously rejected and influenced by the work on GAIM. However this restructuring was still not enough; the NCC decided to remove PC3, but to integrate instead a new attainment target, an amalgamation of the three new targets in the rewritten PC3 into each of the remaining PCs. These were known as 1 and 9 respectively, 'Using and Applying Mathematics', with different titles but identical content. Thus the final structure of attainment targets and PCs could be abbreviated to the following:

PC1:
  1. Using and applying mathematics in number, algebra and measures
  2. Number and number notation
  3. Number operations
  4. Estimation and approximation
  5. Patterns and generalisations
  6. Functions, formulae and equations
  7. Graphical representation
  8. Estimation and measurement

PC2:
  9. Using and applying mathematics in shape and space, and handling data
10. Properties of shapes

11. Location and transformation
12. Collect, record and process data
13. Represent and interpret data
14. Estimate and calculate probabilities

The net effect was considerably to lower the status of the process aspects of mathematics, and to produce two PCs which were inherently unstable and for which a single level would be rather meaningless, each of the two having resulted from a reluctant and arbitrary split in content. There were in compensation a few minor gains in the NCC revision of the mathematics curriculum as a result of the consultation exercise. In the case of 'Using and applying mathematics' (Attainment Targets (ATs) 1 and 9), the content was better expressed and the close relationship with the content targets was made more visible. Under pressure from the National Council for Educational Technology (NCET), more computer-based work was included; the feeling was that it would be more difficult to incorporate it at a later date and that it would act as a pressure on schools both to invest in equipment and to integrate IT into the curriculum.

Although a further concession was made over the multiplication and division of larger numbers without a calculator, the resulting statement included an emphasis on understanding as well as using a method, and avoided the specification of any particular procedure such as long division. The opportunity was taken, again in co-operation with HMI, of adding content to the higher levels and tidying up some examples. However in some cases, in particular the examples for the ATs1 and 9, this only introduced new problems.

Finally the legal requirement for a programme of study again caused problems. There had been considerable opposition in the consultation to the condensed map of the ATs imposed on the working group's report as a panic measure at the last minute. The solution adopted in this version was to make the programme of study a simple transposition of the ATs. The programme of study was thus a copy of the set of statements of attainment, as far as anyone could tell (but not exactly) identical to those listed within the ATs, but listed by target within level, rather than by level within each target. The programme of study was therefore different from those in most other subjects since it was described by level and not by key stage.

The NCC sent their final National Curriculum Drafts for both mathematics and science to the DES in December 1988 (DES/WO, 1988), and after a final statutory and unenthusiastic consultation this version was finally converted almost unchanged into a Statutory Order by Parliament in spring 1989 (DES/WO, 1989a), as an addendum to the 1988 Act. The only significant change in the Statutory Order was the bold reinsertion of the word 'investigation' by the HMI into the description of the targets 'Using and Applying Mathematics'.

The outcome, in essence little changed from the report of the working group, was again generally welcomed, and teachers who were required to implement it starting in September 1989, less than six months from receiving the text, rushed to check their own curriculum schemes against it, looking for omissions that they would have to teach separately.

The NCC had decided to issue non-statutory guidance (NSG) to fit in the ring-binders alongside the statutory orders, aimed at helping teachers with classroom implementation of the new curriculum. A group of progressive educationists and teachers, including some from the working group, were called together by the newly appointed NCC professional mathematics officer, Chris Jones, to discuss what should be issued to assist teachers, and to start on the writing. The result of this conference was heavily rewritten, edited and slimmed down, but nevertheless the opportunity was taken to resurrect the set of radical principles guiding selection of classroom activities which had been part of the original programme of study. Similarly the guidance on calculation strategies and curriculum planning were far more forward looking than the statutory curriculum, and would hardly have been approved of by the Minister and his advisers. This NSG (DES/WO, 1989b) was found reassuring by the Cockcroft-inspired advisory teachers whose job it was initially to co-ordinate the implementation within LEAs.

Indeed the most trenchant criticism of the form of the mathematics national curriculum came initially from educationists, e.g. Howson (1988), Dowling and Noss (1990) and Ernest (1991). Dowling and Noss and Ernest accused members of the working group of compromising their principles in collaborating with a mischievous government in producing a curriculum which was fragmented and reactionary. The response of the working group members would have been that they were only too aware of the compromises, but that these were balanced by some victories for which they had not been credited in subverting some of the original government intentions. Howson attacked from the right rather than the left, mainly aiming at the iniquities of the TGAT framework of age-independent levels, and the resulting equivalence between the curriculum for low-attaining older pupils and high-attaining younger pupils. Again some of this criticism would be readily accepted, but it was unclear that the alternative forms of curriculum differentiation which were then politically feasible were necessarily to be preferred.

THE SECOND VERSION OF THE NC: 1990–92

The reasons for a premature second version

The first version of the NC would very probably still have been in place in 1995 had it not been for the actions of the members and officers of the new School Examinations and Assessment Council (SEAC), who did not really understand the limitations of assessment, either teacher assessment or assessment by standard tasks.

In arriving at 14 attainment targets it had been the views of the Mathematics Working Group that each target represented to some extent an independent strand of mathematical development. It was not therefore unreasonable for teachers to make a judgement about the level to which each pupil had progressed up each strand. The group however recommended that no specific methods of assessment should be imposed and in particular did not suggest that each child should be separately assessed in relation to each statement of attainment. Nevertheless all the publications of SEAC relating to teacher assessment highlighted the importance of assessment of each statement, which led to the encouragement of schools and LEAs to develop complex ticklists.

The SEAC focus on statements of attainment and reporting by AT also caused problems for the design of national tests and for the new NC-related GCSE to be carried out for the first time in 1994, in both mathematics and science. The reports of TGAT and the Mathematics Working Group had emphasised the fact that national assessments (then known as 'standard assessment tasks' (SATs)) should only thinly sample the statements within each of the three (later two) PCs, in order to moderate the more comprehensive results of teacher assessment. However SEAC decisions reflected a political distrust of teacher assessment and hence the desire to use national assessment to provide not just a moderation for each class but also a reliable result for each child. This led to a requirement for GCSE to report separate levels for each AT, and for the SATs to test a large proportion of the statements of attainment in at least some of the targets.

Not surprisingly, the GCSE boards rebelled, claiming reasonably that within the limits of two short examinations they could not report on 14 ATs. They therefore insisted on a reduction in the number of ATs in both mathematics and science. The new Secretary of State, Kenneth Clarke, acquiesced; it is rumoured that agreement was freely given without his realising the extent of consequential disruption for primary as well as for secondary teachers. The opportunity was also seized by SEAC simultaneously to reduce the number of statements of attainment to simplify the teacher assessment ticklists and the complexity of the SATs.

Thus Kenneth Clarke announced in January 1991, less than 18 months after the implementation of the first version, that a second version of the mathematics and science NC would be prepared, for implementation in September 1992. The aim was not to change the content of the curriculum but only the structure.

The NCC had pointed out that the desired results could readily have been achieved without changing the Statutory Order or curriculum documents used by teachers, by a straightforward regrouping of sets of the old ATs into a small number of new targets. The problem of having too many statements of attainment could be dealt with by reversing the originally unintended SEAC emphasis on assessing each statement separately, both in teacher assessment and in SATs. However the relationship between the NCC Chairman and the new

Secretary of State was one of antagonism rather than empathy, and the advice of the NCC was ignored. Not much later the chairmen of both the NCC and SEAC were summarily dismissed by Clarke and replaced by David Pascall and Lord (previously Sir Brian) Griffiths, both members or ex-members of the Central Policy Unit at Downing Street and in sympathy with the right-wing Centre for Policy Studies.

Production and implementation of the second version

Given the level of mistrust of the NCC, there was little alternative but reluctantly to entrust the work of simplification to HMI, restoring the control they had almost lost in previous rounds. The new Staff Inspector in mathematics and an HMI colleague undertook much of the work, consulting with other groups in mathematics education.

Continuity with the previous version was maintained by the shrewd tactic of retaining the previous statements of attainment as the Programme of Study (PoS). The two 'Using and Applying' attainment targets, numbered 1 and 9, were amalgamated into new AT1, with three strands of 'Application', 'Mathematical communication' and 'Reasoning, logic and proof' now separately identified. The opportunity was taken to improve both the statements of attainment and the examples in this area. Thus in some ways the abandoned PC3 was resurrected, perhaps not surprisingly given that the original source of support was from within the HMI. There was no reduction in the number of statements of attainment in the new target, although the statements were no longer repeated twice.

The remaining 12 old ATs were maintained as 'strands' within four new ATs, reflecting generally the coherent areas of content which were previously favoured by the working group as reporting units. However in order to reduce the new ATs to no more than five, the measurement area had to be dismembered and split between the ATs in number and shape. More general statements of attainment were written, many encompassing two or three of the earlier statements. A few statements were either transferred unaltered, or not reflected directly in the new structure. Thus the changes were cosmetic, the number of statements being reduced by about half, but each twice as broad. However there was some increased weight on process and problem-solving.

The ATs were now

1. Using and Applying Mathematics
2. Number
3. Algebra
4. Shape and Space
5. Handling Data

The proposed new Statutory Order for mathematics proceeded smoothly through the stages of consultation with very few changes, was agreed by

Parliament in December 1991 (DES/WO, 1991), and was due to be implemented in September 1992.

A RETROSPECTIVE VIEW

The NCC proposal for a full evaluation of the NC in the core subjects, of which one result was the Mathematics Evaluation Project reported in this book, had been made before Kenneth Clarke's announcement of the second version of the NC in mathematics and science to satisfy the examination boards. The NCC intention was to use the evaluation as the first part of a process aimed to improve significantly the NC at the second iteration. However the NCC proposals lay on ministers' desks so long that by the time agreement was given to the evaluation, teachers were ironically already grappling with an unplanned draft second version.

This timing did not make the Mathematics Evaluation Project any easier, since the curriculum was due to change midway through the two-year project. Thus for the second time politicians pre-empted a proper process of educational evaluation, design and planning, in both cases the premature action resulting in the announcement of a further revision within two years of implementation.

The history of the development of the NC given here highlights the sudden switch in 1987 from a sedate, perhaps overly slow progress towards a national curriculum by consensus, towards a series of rapid ill-planned implementations and revisions, which each time have involved hard-fought battles between different interest groups. The results have been a series of compromise curricula, in which what should have been educational decisions have often been made on political grounds.

The project reported here, Evaluation of the Implementation of National Curriculum Mathematics at Key Stages 1, 2 and 3, took place in 1991–93, in the middle of this turbulent period of curriculum change. The story in relation to relevant events during and after the project will be taken up again in Chapter 6.

2

THE RESEARCH PROGRAMME 1991–93: DATA, DATA ANALYSES AND SELECTED RESULTS

David C. Johnson and Alison Millett
King's College London

BACKGROUND

Following the introduction of the NC in 1989, HMI reports and preliminary NCC monitoring studies revealed four areas of especial concern in the implementation of the NC for mathematics for teachers of pupils in the age range 5–14, KS1, 2 and 3. Particular areas identified were as follows:

1. Difficulties encountered in the implementation of selected topics.
2. Inappropriate progression in the PoS and the ATs.
3. Implementation of AT1 (Ma1), 'Using and Applying Mathematics' (UAM).
4. Effectiveness of the PoS for in-school planning.

In March of 1991 the NCC issued a *Specification to Outside Agencies* for the *Evaluation of the National Curriculum Core Subjects – English, Mathematics and Science at Key Stages 1, 2 and 3* (KS1, 2 and 3). A proposal for a two-year project designed systematically to address the issues and questions related to the concerns indicated for mathematics was submitted by the Centre for Educational Studies, King's College, University of London. The aim of the research was to pursue the four areas indicated above through a connected set of investigations, denoted Studies 1–4 respectively. The project plan included collaboration between staff from the University of London (four), University of Birmingham (one) and the Cambridge Institute of Education (one), i.e. work was to be undertaken in each locality with one member of the project team taking the responsibility for co-ordinating the activity in the region. (Tasks to be undertaken were matched to resources which included percentage time appointments for six researchers, 2.5 full-time equivalent research staff for each year in the two-year period.)

The proposal was successful and work commenced in September 1991. This starting date meant that initial stages of some aspects of the evaluation were based on the 14 ATs in the 1989 Order. As the revised Order, passed in September 1991, primarily involved an amalgamation of these targets, the early activities were judged to be still relevant to the overall programme. However the change of Order led to some added complexity in the interpretation and presentation of results.

As indicated above, the research was designed to encompass issues and concerns related to the four areas. A brief description of the nature of the problems and issues which provided the context and initial work in each of these is given below. Difficulties encountered in the implementation of selected topics (Study 1) focused attention on identifying factors which inhibited (or facilitated) the teaching in those areas of mathematics which HMI and NCC monitoring activities had identified as difficult to implement. Algebra, space and shape and handling data were among those areas particularly noted. The aim was to follow up such concerns as 'conceptual difficulty for pupils', 'teacher's knowledge' of the mathematics curriculum as presented in the Order and resources available or deemed needed, 'meanings teachers attach to the attainment targets (ATs) and corresponding statements of attainment (SoAs)', and 'the degree to which teachers were differentiating curricula and organising their teaching', with a view to providing practical guidance to teachers and advice to the NCC.

Progression in the PoS and the ATs (Study 2) arose from the concern that the structure for the ATs, statements of attainment (SoAs) and the PoS reflected some degree of 'inappropriate progression'. The investigation involved a detailed analysis of the sequencing of SoAs and consistency in the implied developmental model for curriculum planning. A systematic review was conducted of the SoAs within each of the new ATs, Ma2–5, and PoS for the relevant key stages. Data and examples from classes or individual pupils, and evidence of teachers' interpretations of the statements, were collected to support the findings and recommendations.

Implementation of Ma1, 'Using and Applying Mathematics' (Study 3); focused on aspects of teaching for this attainment target (UAM). Initial work was on the meanings or interpretations teachers gave to the AT. This was followed with case studies of a selected set of teachers deemed to provide exemplars of practices employed in the integration of UAM throughout the school mathematics curriculum.

Effectiveness of the PoS for in-school planning (Study 4) involved a consideration of the nature of whole-school/department and individual teacher planning and associated review procedures, especially the extent to which teachers were basing these on NC documents. The effectiveness of the PoS as a basis

NCC Spec

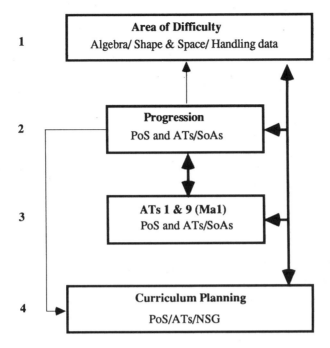

Figure 2.1 Mathematics KS1, 2, 3. Organisation – the four linked studies

for planning and their relationship with the SoAs provided an initial focus. This was extended to include other aspects of planning and implementation, e.g. the role of commercial/published schemes and other materials as mediators of the NC and the inclusion of cross-curricular activities and differentiation.

The research began with a relatively clear focus – the NCC specification and the plan to link the four studies. The model employed was that of two members of the research team having primary responsibility for a given study, but with data collection in each study designed to inform all four – see Figure 2.1. However, there were a number of important influences which affected the work at different stages. Two main influences were

- new and important considerations suggested by the data (some aspects of these were included in the final report and also provide the basis for Chapters 3–5 in this book); and
- the 'changing goal-posts' – shifts in concerns, in particular the need to deal with current or new issues as identified by the funding agency, the NCC.

Relative to the second point above, the contract required interim reports to be produced at six-month intervals over the two-year period. It was also the case that the research team was asked to address some of the new or current issues in a particular interim report, and ultimately the Final Report, even though this was not directly alluded to in the main areas described in the initial specification. An example here is the concern for 'manageability' identified in the latter part of the 1991–92 school year – it was noticed that primary teachers in particular were expressing concern about coping with the Orders across the range of school subjects. The project team was asked to address aspects of this issue specific to school mathematics in the September 1992 Interim Report, and again in the Final Report (for example the report included a section entitled 'Slimming the curriculum?').

We hasten to add here that such shifts were not unexpected nor should they have been as the contract issued did note this possibility. Hence, while the four studies might in some ways have appeared to have been restricted in their potential for providing evidence across a wider field, the research methodology and data collection were designed to enable new issues and ideas to emerge. As such this also enabled the team to respond in some way to the new requests – but in many cases this could only be done through making inferences from a related, but not necessarily planned and/or directly linked, data set. This important aspect of conducting contract research for governmental agencies will be illustrated further in a later section in this chapter – 'Themes, issues and recommendations' – and picked up again in Chapter 6.

METHODOLOGY

A variety of methodologies was identified as appropriate to each area of the evaluation. The main sources of data for Studies 1 and 4 (difficulties and planning respectively) were from survey questionnaires and follow-up interviews from a national sample. Study 2 (sequencing and progression) utilised the judgements and advice from selected groups of teachers meeting regularly over the two-year period of the study, and the work for Study 3 (implementation of Ma1) through a small number of case studies. Data from the questionnaires and interviews were also used to inform Studies 2 and 3. Other data sources included meetings with LEA advisory staff and contacts with publishers, Inset providers and HMI, along with reports, published and unpublished, from other projects and monitoring activities. The main data sources are summarised in Table 2.1 and these are described further in the following sections.

The questionnaire

Development

The initial stage in the development of the questionnaire involved informal contacts with teachers representing KS1, 2 and 3. They were asked to express their opinions in four main areas:

Table 2.1 Data collection

Source	Summary of data collection
Questionnaire	Distributed to 100 teachers in each of 11 LEAs, 68% teacher response rate with 75% of the schools represented. Full data set of 744 responses was analysed, initially by key stage. SoA data was obtained from 659 responses from teachers. Further requirements for analysis were then identified on the basis of an analysis of the interviews (see below) and these resulted in the selection of cross-tabulations appropriate to each of the four studies
Interviews	32 teachers were interviewed, representing all year groups in KS1, 2 and 3. Interviews were also held with headteachers (primary) or heads of mathematics departments (secondary) in all the schools; 30 teacher interviews were transcribed (two tapes were unusable) and the transcriptions coded according to a scheme generated from initial reviews and linked to the four studies
Teacher groups	Two teacher groups were established, one in the Cambridge area and one in the Birmingham area. Each group comprised four teachers from each of two LEAs; 15 monthly teacher-group meetings were held. An additional one day per month for each teacher was devoted to classroom-based research activity. Data collected included work from pupils and from colleagues in teachers' schools, and these along with relevant literature/reports (see 'documents/reports' below) represented important components in the analyses
Case studies	Case-study methodology was employed to gain an impression of the range of practices of teachers (24) who were engaged in the implementation of Ma1 and to identify a small group of teachers (six–two from each KS) to follow up further. This follow-up activity involved both classroom observation and interviews. Field notes and tape recordings of interviews and teacher and pupil interactions provided the main data for analysis
Advisers' meetings	A meeting was held with each of 10 out of the 11 LEA advisers' groups co-operating with the project. The discussion at these meetings was structured in terms of a common framework of themes and questions
Contact with publishers	Publishers of mathematics materials were contacted and each was asked to complete a brief questionnaire on present and future publications. Ten major publishers were consulted further with extended interviews conducted with two – involved in the development of new, but at that time unpublished, schemes, one primary and one secondary
Inset providers	Tutors for the 56 '20-day' inservice courses being conducted in the school year 1992–93 were contacted and asked to respond to an open question regarding their assessment of the course participants' confidence and subject knowledge for each of the ATs Ma1–5. Responses were received from 20 tutors
Contact with HMI	An informal meeting to discuss the broad themes/issues addressed by the project was held with the Staff Inspector, Mathematics
Documents/reports	The work also drew upon a number of other (current) reports and ongoing projects and the data collected for these reports and projects. The literature base included research reports/papers/books, curriculum development project outcomes, government reports, reports from professional associations and evaluation studies relating to the implementation of assessment requirements for the mathematics curriculum

- Difficulties which they were experiencing in implementing the NC.
- Their use and familiarity with the NC documents.
- The detail in which they would be willing to comment on the various components of the NC.
- The kinds of support they would welcome.

The initial discussions with these teachers indicated variations in areas of difficulty and suggested reasons for these. Reasons given ranged from the more practical matters of classroom organisation, through lack of teacher knowledge and experience, to lack of understanding of some parts of the documents, particularly SoAs, and anxieties about sequencing and levels. Concern was also expressed about what was perceived as an inadequacy of some aspects of the documents. These were all deemed important for consideration in the construction of the questionnaire.

The variation in teachers' familiarity with the NC documents was wide, indicating that this was an area which needed to be probed in the questionnaire. Different documents, and parts of documents, were more highly valued by different teachers with noticeable variation between primary and secondary. There was also variation in the extent to which they would feel able to comment on details of the documents. However, it was clear from several of the teachers that they would welcome the opportunity to comment at the level of AT, with some teachers expressing quite clear views on specific SoAs. Different practices in type and frequency of planning were noted. The views on help which had been of value were also of use and provided ideas for questions in this area. Practical help provided by the LEA was mentioned specifically by one group of teachers and the need for Inset in specific areas was also suggested.

The project team incorporated these inputs, along with issues raised in reports and materials currently available from the NCC and DES, into the initial planning of the structure of the questionnaire. The model for the development of the questionnaire involved an interaction between the research team in the preparation of questions, initially in an open 'ask what you feel should be asked' situation, which in turn contributed to an evolving structure and further preparation, refinement and 'clustering' of questions.

A pilot version of the questionnaire was trialled with 25 primary and 12 secondary teachers (with the secondary teachers asked to invite other teachers in their departments to participate). Results indicated that a number of modifications were necessary, most dealing with the length and complexity of some items. One main modification was to reduce a question which asked respondents to review all SoAs across all 14 ATs so as to include only one or two ATs.

The final questionnaire comprised nine sections, with a total of 39 questions, excluding background information, with a number of subitems for each question. As trialling indicated that the resulting document was still long, taking about 45 minutes to one hour to complete, the questionnaire was produced in two parts, with an indication that the respondent would not have to complete both in 'one go'. A copy of the final questionnaire is given in Appendix 1. The questionnaire returns were coded for optical mark reading and computer processing of the data.

Sample

Eleven LEAs participated in this part of the project. These were selected (through personal contact and invitation) to provide a reasonable national distribution in terms of a spread across the country and in terms of the availability of inner-city, suburban and rural area schools. Metropolitan, inner-city areas from the north, the Midlands and the south were represented, as were more prosperous suburban areas and rural areas with small schools, as well as small towns and county towns. Examples were provided of different types of organisation, as well as a variety of inner-city, urban and rural schools in a more prosperous part of the country.

Using information provided by each of the 11 LEAs, the schools were categorised by status, type and size (primary schools) and by status, type, selective/non-selective, age range, sex and size for the secondary schools. Schools were selected randomly from the list of schools in the authority, and assigned to the appropriate category and subcategory. The proportion of schools in each category in the population for the LEA was reflected as accurately as possible in the sample.

The final questionnaire was sent to 100 teachers in each of the 11 authorities. While the schools were contacted to obtain agreement to participate, the teachers were randomly chosen within each school according to a prescribed sampling plan. To provide as wide a spread of schools as possible, but still keeping the sample to manageable proportions, two teachers from each school received the questionnaire, selected according to year group (for the purpose of the study, the year groups were Reception through to Yr9). On some occasions, because of the age of transfer, it was necessary to select three teachers from middle schools, and only one from secondary 13–18.

In a sample of 50 schools in each authority, 35 covered the primary range (R through to Yr6) and 15 covered the secondary range (Yr7–9). Seventy primary teachers and 30 secondary teachers received the questionnaire, except in the case of authorities with age of transfer at 13. In some small authorities with fewer than 15 secondary schools, three questionnaires were sent to each school.

The year groups from R through to Yr9 were covered, 10 teachers of each year group being selected from each LEA. A variety of combinations of year groups (e.g. R, Yr4) was used. Headteachers were asked to hand the questionnaire to a teacher of the specified year group (or whose class contained that year group), with instructions to choose the second alphabetically if there was more than one such teacher.

Before the questionnaire was administered, 18 schools out of the original 543 approached had indicated, either to their LEA maths adviser or directly to the project, that they were unwilling to participate. These schools were replaced with schools in the same category. After the questionnaire was distributed, a further eight schools withdrew their co-operation, and these were again replaced with reserves where possible. Where this was not possible, extra questionnaires were sent to teachers in the appropriate year groups in other schools which had already agreed to participate. Reasons given for non-participation included: other initiatives or exams going on in the school; too many demands being made on teachers at the moment; selection for participation in other surveys; staff changes and overload of probationary teachers; a move towards grant-maintained status; a lack of confidence in any notice being taken of teachers' opinions; and uncertainty as to whether the school had agreed to participate in the project.

Respondents

Questionnaires were returned from 744 teachers, a 68 per cent response rate representing 75 per cent of the schools. The questionnaire response by year group reflected the intended distribution to a considerable extent (10 per cent of the questionnaires being sent to each year group, R to Yr9). The response from all year groups fell within the range 9–11 per cent of the total, the lowest being 9 per cent for Yr1, 2 and 3 and the highest being 11 per cent for R, Yr7, 8 and 9, the remaining three year groups contributing 10 per cent each. As the questionnaires were distributed over 11 LEAs, about 9 per cent went to each authority. The response rates from the different authorities varied from 7 per cent of the total to 11 per cent of the total.

The distribution of questionnaires to the three key stages was 30 per cent to KS1, 40 per cent to KS2 and 30 per cent to KS3. The questionnaires returned show that 32 per cent of the respondents were teaching in KS3, a slightly higher response rate than from the other two key stages; KS1 responses comprised 29 per cent of the total and KS2 responses comprised 39 per cent of the total.

The great majority of the respondents (96 per cent) had permanent status within their schools, with 3 per cent indicating that they had temporary status, and fewer than 1 per cent being supply teachers. Two per cent of the respondents were part-time teachers.

The types of schools from which the respondents came corresponded closely with those in the sample, schools with 100–249 pupils being slightly under-represented, and schools with over 750 pupils being slightly over-represented. Primary/combined and 11–18 schools were slightly under-represented and 11–16 schools slightly over-represented. Twenty-eight per cent of the schools were categorised by the teachers as being in inner-city areas, 22 per cent in other urban areas, 28 per cent in suburban areas and 22 per cent were categorised as rural schools.

Of the respondents who answered the question on gender, 68 per cent were female and 32 per cent were male, although the proportions differed considerably from one key stage to another – 98 per cent female and 2 per cent male in KS1, 69 per cent female and 31 per cent male in KS2, and 41 per cent female and 59 per cent male in KS3.

The majority of the respondents were experienced teachers – 72 per cent across all three key stages had 10 or more years of teaching experience. Three per cent of the respondents were in their first year of teaching, 2 per cent had one year's teaching experience, 11 per cent had taught for 2–5 years and 12 per cent had taught for 5–10 years. Ninety-six per cent of KS3 teachers had 'teaching maths' as a main focus in their teacher training.

The interviews

Subsample

Teachers were asked in the questionnaire whether they would be willing to be interviewed in the second stage of the project. Between 25 and 30 per cent of teachers indicated that they would be prepared to be interviewed, with a greater number of secondary teachers volunteering.

Criteria for selection were established, linked to responses to selected items in the questionnaire, and a subset of 33 teachers was identified for interview. The criteria used were based on

- differing frequency of use of NC documents (high, medium, low);
- differing emphasis on cross-curricular work – primary (high, medium, low); and
- differing emphasis on Ma1, UAM – secondary (high, low).

This selection procedure provided nine categories for primary teachers and six categories for secondary teachers. At least one teacher was selected from each category, and there were at least two teachers from each year group in the sample.

The intention was to select teachers to represent a variety of different types of planning and delivery of the mathematics curriculum. Hence, as indicated above, the interview sample was a well defined selected subset of those teachers who agreed to be interviewed, and was not intended to be random or fully representative of the questionnaire sample or the population as a whole. It was also the case that the sample was taken from a subset of the LEAs. For each school represented in the interview sample, interviews were also conducted with the head (primary) or the head of department (HoD) (secondary).

The interview schedule

The interview stage following the initial analysis of questionnaire data drew upon identified areas of interest from the questionnaire responses. The use of the interview was to illuminate questionnaire responses and probe more deeply into areas of particular concern in the NCC specification for each of the four studies.

Interview schedules were developed by the project team using an interactive model similar to that employed in the construction of the questionnaire. The schedules contained questions relating not only to Studies 1 and 4, difficulties and planning respectively, but also to Study 2, sequencing and progression, and Study 3, the implementation of Ma1. The schedules for both teachers and headteachers or HoDs were trialled in the first three joint interviews, i.e. two project research officers were present, and post-interview review indicated there was no need for amendment in content, but did suggest changes in layout/sequence. To ensure consistency in the use of the schedule, each member of the team who participated in interviewing took part in a joint interview with another member of the team.

Post-interview procedure

Thirty-two interviews were completed (one interviewee was on long-term sick leave). The interviews with teachers were transcribed and returned to the teachers for validation/clarification. Transcripts were also annotated to clarify points (e.g. documents being referred to) by the member of the team who conducted the interview. The interviews with heads or HoDs were primarily for background and further illumination. They were not transcribed. The quality of two interview tapes was very poor, and consequently 30 transcribed interviews were available for analysis.

A post-interview procedure was discussed at team meetings and agreed upon. This also included instructions for completing forms related to an 'interview impression', an 'interview summary' and a questionnaire/interview comparison.

A set of coding categories was established, derived initially from the focus of questions in the interviews, and modified after trial use on a sample of interview transcripts. The coding schedule comprised 28 categories for analysis. These ranged from a consideration of document use through classroom organisation and teaching strategies, differentiation and progression, difficulties, constraints, UAM, needs, changes and beliefs, etc. (The full listing is given in Appendix 2.) Additional categories developed from further analysis of data in the four studies.

The teacher groups – Study 2, sequencing and progression

Two teachers' groups were set up to support Study 2, with eight teachers in each group comprising four teachers from each of two LEAs. Fifteen monthly teacher-group meetings were held over the two-year period. An additional one day per month for each teacher was devoted to classroom-based research activity (this was a negotiated and agreed minimal level of commitment).

The teachers were selected with the support of the local advisory teams. The two co-ordinators met regularly to ensure a parallel programme for each group. The members of the team carrying out this study worked with the 1991 Orders (draft from September 1991, final from January 1992) and collected evidence on the structure and content. The task for the groups was to consider those aspects of sequencing and progression in the PoS and SoAs which might be deemed 'inappropriate'.

The teacher research groups were working with evidence gathered from

- examples of pupils' work (across the key stages) to consider the match between planning and outcomes;
- discussion with colleagues in the teachers' own schools on their perspectives of the NC, its interpretation and implementation;
- identification of, and written reflection on, relevant aspects of the teachers' own practice, followed by discussion and elaboration within the groups;
- research literature and curriculum development reports related to specific areas of mathematics and which offered some indications or insights in regard to sequencing and progression in learning;
- SATs test data for each of the three key stages (where available); and
- results from the project questionnaire.

Typically, at each meeting, the teachers considered certain of the SoAs or aspects of the PoS which had been selected as a focus for discussion. This led to a consideration of

- meanings that could be attached to statements,
- expected levels of response from pupils,
- the development of progression through the levels,
- consistency within a level,
- the relationship of PoS to SoAs,
- the use of, and progression within, the strands, and
- the appropriateness and range of the examples.

A range of classroom tasks was devised according to the purpose of the particular meeting and carried out with pupils covering the first three key stages. Pupils' work was analysed and moderated so as to aid in the analyses of a developmental progression in terms of attainment identified by the teachers.

At each stage the teacher researchers recorded their findings using a proforma requiring further written information about pupil activity and discussions with colleagues. Pupil activity was also exemplified through an annotated sample of pupil work. These data formed the basis for both discussion and the development of the enquiry at each group meeting. At every stage the teachers' findings were discussed and analysed in relation to the sequencing and progression in the strands defined by the NC.

Near the end of the project, and after participation in the 15 monthly meetings, the two groups met together with other teachers from Study 3 (see below) and the full project team for a weekend conference. The focus of the working conference was to produce a synthesis of the issues raised within and across the five ATs (Ma1–5).

The case studies – Study 3, implementation of Ma1 (UAM)

Selection of the case-study teachers

Two groups of people were used to aid in the identification of (potential) case-study classrooms:

- Advisory staff in three LEAs were asked to identify schools and teachers they considered were developing promising approaches to Ma1.
- Teachers involved in an earlier NCC Using and Applying Mathematics Project were followed up (resulting in the decision to add another LEA to the initial set).

As a result nine teachers were contacted in the first instance. Interviews were arranged with these teachers and, where possible, lessons observed. There were two aims to this initial contact:

- To begin to identify ways in which Ma1 was being incorporated into the mathematics curriculum.
- To formulate criteria for the selection of teachers to be followed up further.

The initial group was then extended to include 24 teachers, and case-study methodology was employed to gain an impression of the range of practices of these teachers and ultimately the selection of a small group of teachers (six – two from each key stage) to follow up further.

The data

The principal sources of data were field notes, participant observation of lessons and interviews with the teachers and in some cases the pupils. Lessons were observed on a number of occasions; each lasted at least an hour (apart from one KS3 single, 35-minute lesson), some covered an entire morning. The pattern of data gathering was varied to begin to provide some depth as well as breadth. For example two classrooms were visited for every mathematics lesson over the course of a week; a KS3 class was visited at each of the different times that they had mathematics lessons; other classrooms were 'dipped into'. Field notes taken at the time of observing were written up and expanded. In some cases tape recordings of teacher and pupil interactions were made and selected portions of these transcribed. Wherever possible the lessons observed were immediately followed up with teacher interviews focused on significant aspects of the particular lesson. The teachers were also interviewed on more general aspects of their teaching such as planning and record keeping and their perceptions of the role of Ma1.

Field notes and tape recordings of interviews and teacher and pupil interactions provided the main data for analyses.

Advisers' meetings

Informal group meetings were scheduled to be held between project staff and the advisory staff in each of the 11 LEAs during the early stages of the project. Due to difficulties in scheduling, these were only held with 10 of the LEA advisers' groups. For the majority of the meetings two project research officers were in attendance and the discussion was structured in terms of a common framework of themes and questions – appropriate to each of the four areas being investigated as well as addressing issues which cut across the studies. A general guideline for the meeting was prepared by the project team – it is noted here, however, that the guideline was not intended to direct or lead the discussion, but rather was there to provide some focus (and a reminder) as to the points which might be discussed.

A report on each of the meetings was written up from notes and, where appropriate, agreed as a reasonable account by the two team members present (these were not returned to advisers for comment). The reports represented a further complementary data set for informing the work.

Contact with publishers

Publishers of mathematics materials and commercial schemes were contacted and were asked to complete a brief questionnaire on present and future publications. Ten major publishers were consulted further, and asked to provide more details on materials specific to particular themes in the study, e.g. Ma1, progression, differentiation, cross-curricular activities and variations in approaches.

Two publishers were identified from the responses for further interview on the basis that they were involved in the development of new, but at that time unpublished, schemes, one primary and one secondary. The interviews were conducted by two project officers and each lasted half a day. The interview was informal and no specific guidelines were prepared (beyond a preparatory discussion of points which might be raised by the two project team members). Reports on the two interviews were written up and agreed by the two project members who conducted the interviews (the same two people participated in each).

In addition, reviews, published or commissioned by the project, of eight widely used schemes were collected to support the analyses, in particular the work of Study 2, sequencing and progression.

Contact with Inset providers

Tutors for the 56 '20-day' inservice courses being conducted in the school year 1992–93 were contacted (in January 1993) and asked to respond to an open question regarding their assessment of the course participants' knowledge and understanding relative to each of the ATs Ma1–5. A 'comments' form was provided, including space for any other points/observations they might wish to raise. Responses were received from 20 tutors and the data from these were used to inform aspects of Study 1, difficulties, Study 3, implementation of Ma1, and the final chapter, 'Themes and Recommendations', Chapter 6 in the Final Report (Askew *et al.*, 1993).

Contact with HMI

An informal meeting to discuss the broad themes/issues addressed by the project was held with the Staff Inspector, Mathematics. In addition, information and insights were shared relative to HMI monitoring exercises and the project draft interim reports (three) – with an understanding from both parties that any unpublished information was to be considered confidential until such time as it was 'officially' released.

Documents/reports

The work also drew upon a number of other current or recently published reports and ongoing projects and the data collected for these reports and projects. Examples of these include the following:

- Reports on the implementation of the NC from the NCC (1991), HMI (1991a; 1991b; 1992a; 1992b), Ofsted (1993a; 1993b; 1993c; 1993d) and the professional associations – ASE/ATM/MA/NATE (1989; 1990; 1992).
- Data resulting from national assessment in its pilot or operational forms from ENCA Project/Leeds (SEAC, 1992), NFER/BGC (1991; 1992) and CATS/King's College London (1990; 1991; 1992).
- Reports on other work deemed relevant, e.g. Alexander, Rose and Woodhead (1992) and NCC (1992).
- Relevant research, e.g. the work of 1) the CSMS Project (Hart, 1981); 2) the Strategies and Errors in Secondary Mathematics (SESM) Project – ratio (Hart, 1984), algebra (Booth, 1984), fractions (Kerslake, 1986) and graphs

(Sharma, 1993); and 3) the Children's Mathematical Frameworks (CMF) Project (Johnson, 1989).

SELECTED FINDINGS FROM THE FOUR STUDIES

Detailed discussions of the findings and data used to support these are given in the full report (Askew *et al.*, 1993). The following subsections represent 'snapshots' of selected aspects of the results from each of the four studies to provide a link to the remaining chapters in this book.

Effectiveness of the PoS for in-school planning (Study 4)

The main data for this study were from the questionnaires, the interviews, input from meetings with mathematics advisory teams and information collected from publishers of mathematics materials. The initial focus, that of the degree to which the PoS was used as a basis for planning, was extended in the development of the questionnaire to include other aspects of planning and implementation – e.g. the role of published schemes and other materials as mediators of the NC, as well as cross-curricular activities and differentiation.

Part 1 of the questionnaire (see Appendix 1) contained questions almost entirely related to planning and associated areas of coverage and recording. The first two questions dealt with organisation for mathematics teaching. These were intended to indicate the approach/es used by the teacher to address differentiation and thus set the following planning questions in context. Teachers were asked in the second section about the frequency of their planning and the degree of collaboration with other teachers as well as about the range and frequency of planning documents used. The third section, questions 6–14, focused on the relative use of the various components in the NC documents – ATs, SoAs, PoS and the NSG. Using resources/classroom materials, which included the use of commercial schemes, was the major focus in the fourth section and the degree of cross-curricular work and strategies for coverage and review comprised the next two sections. Part 1 ended with a short section on UAM and ways of planning for this.

Aspects of the questionnaire items and other areas of interest relevant to each of the four studies were followed up with the interview subsample (using a style of open questions but within a well defined interview schedule).

Findings

Some general points which emerged from the data were

- comments on the 1991 NC Order as a whole were generally favourable as regards planning;

- the 10-level scale was regarded as helpful (interview finding);
- for many teachers the PoS (in the 1989 Order) played a very minor role in their planning; and
- time was needed to digest, evaluate and deal with the complexity of the mathematics NC; time for teachers to work together and to develop school schemes of work.

Outcomes of particular relevance to Chapter 3 in this book include

- the major role in planning for many teachers was taken by the commercial scheme – that is, the degree of (commercial) scheme use and the way that the scheme was used were major influences on the way in which teachers planned their teaching for mathematics;
- some teachers relied almost entirely on a commercial scheme for differentiation, with varying degrees of intervention;
- the use of commercial schemes increased through the key stages, from KS1 to KS3; and
- with the above said, it was also the case that many teachers used a commercial scheme as only one of a range of planning resources – these teachers also made use of NC documents, school schemes of work and other non-scheme mathematics resources.

Difficulties encountered in the implementation of selected topics (Study 1)

The main data for this study were the questionnaires (Part 2, questions 33–36), interviews and aspects of the work of the teacher groups in Study 2. Outcomes from the questionnaire were only considered when percentages of 10 per cent or more of the respondents indicated difficulty in a particular area of mathematics. Using this criteria, note must be made of the fact that in many instances a substantial majority of the teachers did not indicate the particular area to be one of 'perceived difficulty', i.e. the findings represented an important input to the issues, but one could not generalise these to any 'large' percentage of teachers.

Findings

Some general points which emerged from the data were as follows:

- The data generally confirmed the findings presented in earlier monitoring studies – teachers' perceptions reported by the evaluation were that their difficulties lay in three main areas; those of 'Using and Applying Mathematics' (Ma1), handling data (Ma5) and algebra (Ma3).
- It was also noted that in contrast to earlier monitoring, shape and space (Ma4) was not perceived as an area which was particularly difficult to

implement. However, Chapter 4 presents a different side to this coin. Perceptions may well have been affected by the fact that the language in the AT is familiar; it was only after careful study of the SoAs (by the teacher groups in Study 2) that the problems became apparent.

Of particular interest in the research were the teachers' perceived reasons for the difficulties. These included

- difficulties associated with 'too much to get through';
- lack of experience or lack of confidence in own knowledge;
- lack of availability or adequacy of resources;
- difficulties with using the documents – e.g. lack of clarity in the meaning of some SoAs (this is picked up again in Chapter 4 – the work of the teacher groups in Study 2, sequencing and progression); and
- difficulties with making provision for different levels of attainment, particularly at KS2.

Selected aspects of the above are also addressed in Chapter 3.

Progression in the PoS and the ATs (Study 2)

The work of the two teacher groups over the two-year period is described in Chapter 4. For this reason, only a few outcomes are presented here to provide an indication of how the four studies were linked and in turn how this enabled the research team to come to address other issues and themes.

Findings

Particular points which emerged were as follows:

- the PoS as presented (in the 1991 Order) did not appear to offer a coherent working model for curriculum planning.
- The presentation of mathematics in the Order was seen to produce a view of the nature of the subject as made up of completely isolated content blocks.
- Concern was expressed that the national tests, with short and mainly written items, could lead to a narrowing of the curriculum.
- IT was considered to have a great deal to offer in supporting learning and teaching in mathematics – however, the emphasis in the Order, when it occurs, is placed on 'using the tools' and what is intended to constitute appropriate use of IT tools for any particular statement in the PoS or SoAs was difficult to discern.
- Despite the many concerns resulting from this investigation, the teacher groups decided that it was not desirable nor necessary to rewrite the curriculum immediately.

- However, in the long term a revised NC Order should take more account of teacher needs for effective planning. One suggested way forward was to move to a key-staged PoS for mathematics.

Implementation of Ma1 (UAM) (Study 3)

As the intended outcome for this study was to provide examples of 'promising' teaching practice in the implementation of UAM (as described in the NSG), the main data for this purpose were the observations and interviews from the six case-study teachers. However, the brief taken on by the research team was much broader and included a consideration of teachers' interpretations of, or the meanings they attached to, this AT. Hence, the analyses included data from the questionnaire (in particular, the last section in Part 1 and those aspects of each of the questions in Part 2 related to UAM), the interview subsample, the meetings with advisory teachers, information from publishers and the case-study teachers. The findings were then presented in two parts – 'teachers' interpretation and implementation' and 'promising practice'. The focus of Chapter 5 is on the first of these areas – with more detailed information provided relative to the seven bullet points given below.

Findings – teachers' interpretation and implementation

- Teachers interviewed displayed wide variation in their interpretation of Ma1, UAM. In turn this appeared to have affected their style and extent of implementation. The title of the AT seemed to have led many of the teachers to believe that by providing mathematics lessons in which materials were used or reference was made to the 'real world', pupils must be engaged in Ma1. Although such a view was most likely to be expressed by KS1 teachers, this perception was not unique to them.
- Ma1 appeared often to have been interpreted in ways which fitted with current practice and presented minimal need for change.
- Very few of the teachers interviewed spoke about attainment in UAM which indicated any degree of familiarity with the relevant SoAs.
- Although questionnaire responses indicated a high degree of planning for Ma1 (and a correspondingly high percentage of classroom time spent on this AT), the interview data indicated that there was little specific planning for this AT. At KS3 what was done was often in terms of providing contexts for assessment rather than for teaching.
- The interview teachers frequently mentioned the use of practical work as a means of implementing Ma1. Many of the examples provided (by the teachers) had a sense of starting with a piece of mathematical content and then finding some means of making it 'practical' either by involving physical materials, diagrams or devising some sort of 'real world' context. Under this

interpretation, practical work is closer to being a teaching context than one requiring pupils to use and apply mathematics.

- The models of Ma1 presented by some commercial schemes may reinforce a limited interpretation of this AT; in particular the erroneous belief that any mention of the 'real world' must necessarily invoke Ma1.
- The presentation of problem-solving and investigative activities in some commercial schemes could be taken as suggesting these were primarily for the more able pupil, i.e. extension activities for those who have completed the core work.

Findings – promising practice

Interviews and classroom observations of the six case-study teachers led to the identification of six principles as providing an implicit framework for their practice:

- Teaching for strategies associated with Ma1 is both possible and appropriate.
- Ma1 is a means of both applying and developing understanding of the content of Ma2–5 (as noted in the NSG).
- All pupils have skills and understanding in UAM to build upon.
- Pupils explaining and justifying are central to Ma1 at all ages and levels.
- UAM both requires and develops pupils' abilities to sustain engagement with activities.
- UAM as defined by Ma1 is reflective, requiring and promoting mental activity.

Vignettes which illustrate each of these principles are given in the Final Report (Askew *et al.*, 1993, Chapter 5).

THEMES, ISSUES AND RECOMMENDATIONS

The findings from the four interlinked studies, linked through the sharing of data collected and the range of methodologies employed as each study had its specific focus, were drawn together to address a broader set of themes and issues. These, while implied in the specification from the NCC, went beyond those identified in the initial proposal in that they reflected thinking and concerns at the end of the project, July 1993, which had emerged from the data and from the (by-then) 'current' concerns, policies and practices of the agencies involved, NCC and SEAC – soon to be merged into one, the (at that time) new School Curriculum and Assessment Authority (SCAA).

Themes and issues

The aims of the NC are expressed in terms of the entitlement of all pupils to a broad and balanced curriculum, and to development in their learning (DES,

1989). The most critical factor in achieving this aim is clearly the nature of the *pupils' classroom experience*. A major influence on the nature of the pupils' experience is *the teacher*, who has the responsibility of interpreting *the Order* and translating it into a set of classroom activities. However, the teacher's planning and implementation must also be considered in the *culture and context* of the school and the community. The model selected for the synthesis of the results of the research was therefore to consider these four focal points (see Figure 2.2). These were not intended to represent disjoint or unique areas, but were selected to provide a means for structuring the discussion in our attempt to address the emerging issues and concerns.

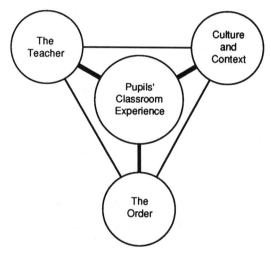

Figure 2.2   The model used in the synthesis of the results

It was the research team's opinion that the interconnections among these four elements needed to be considered both in understanding any changes that had taken place as a result of the NC, and in the planning for future changes. Our position was/is that the way in which teachers, headteachers, test-writers, publishers, parents and pupils interpret the Order, in relation to the context and culture in which they are working, is more important than the nature of the Order itself.

The Final Report (Askew *et al.*, 1993) presented the evidence and implications from our work under the four headings, with attention given to those aspects for which we had at least complementary evidence. The points addressed included the following (NB: The number in square brackets at the end of selected items links these to subsequent chapters in this book).

The mathematics Order

- Changes to the statutory Order – when and how? – the need for a period of stability and time to trial new ideas. [4]

- Problems arising out of the dual nature of the (then) current mathematics Order as attempting to fulfil the requirements of providing both a framework to guide teaching and a prescription for assessment arrangements. [4]
- The need for an alternative presentation of the PoS as a basis for coherent key-stage-related planning. [4]
- Slimming the curriculum? The need to retain breadth and balance.
- The ATs and the need for further exemplification of the SoAs – however, the interpretation of any Order would not be determined simply by the words on the page, but by the collective wisdom of teachers, authors, test-writers and others. [4]
- The importance of Ma1 and the need for support in the integration of Ma1 with teaching and assessing Ma2–5. [5]
- Benefits of and difficulties with the 10-level scale – provides a framework against which pupils' attainment and progress can be assessed, but presentation may lead to teaching mathematics 'level by level'. [3, 4]
- The failure (at that point in time) of the recommendations in the NSG to permeate the system in any explicit way – valued by those familiar with the document, but not consulted by many teachers. [5]

The teacher

- The process and rate of change; the importance of collaborative work in planning; the opportunity to 'try things out'; and 'the long road to ownership'. [4]
- The importance of subject knowledge and a 'holistic' view of the mathematics curriculum.
- The important role and potential benefit of teacher assessment used both formatively and summatively, provided the balance between end-of-key-stage results in national tests and in teacher assessment is fair.
- The role (and type) of professional development (inservice and initial training) provision suitable for supporting the implementation of the 'intended' curriculum and the important role of mathematics advisory staff in this endeavour.

Culture and context

- Parental expectations – the importance of parental awareness of the full range of mathematical outcomes described in the documents.
- Whole-school policy and procedures for supporting activities for enhancing or facilitating the implementation of the curriculum.
- LEA, HE and Office for Standards in Education (Ofsted) support – the need for personnel with responsibility for, and experience and expertise in, mathematics, and the important role of LEA advisory staff and HE lecturers involved in inservice and initial training in providing a network for selection and dissemination of advice and guidance.

- Professional associations – an important channel for communication and advice.
- Publishers – the need for a period of stability and consolidation in a period of uncertainty and concern. [3]

Pupils' classroom experiences

- The need to address issues of the nature of the content and organisation of mathematics schemes and the way teachers use schemes. [3]
- Curriculum organisation and the use of a theme/modular approach – facilitating more coherence in the curriculum and a better chance of incorporating Ma1 into the other content targets as well as integrating work across targets. [3, 5]
- Differentiation – providing appropriate experiences, even when grouping/ setting continues to present problems for many teachers and possibly even more so if one wishes to maximise the potential of all pupils ('raising standards'). [3]
- Pupils' expectations in *learning* mathematics – empowerment would seem to come through a breadth of experience. [3]

Recommendations

The findings from the four studies and the themes and issues which cut across the four areas led to the presentation of 17 Recommendations. The report was accepted as fulfilling the conditions of the contract. However, recommendations seldom provide the 'right' answers, nor should they be taken to do so – ideas are put forward for discussion and debate. 'Moving goal-posts' being a feature of the policies of the day were taken up by the debate at ministerial level and we found ourselves reporting at the time discussions and deliberations were leading to the Dearing review (see Chapter 6). Shortly after completing the final report the project team submitted a written 'Response to Sir Ronald Dearing from the NCC Maths Evaluation Project' (see Appendix 3). This represented an abbreviated version of the findings and themes, issues and Recommendations as given in the main report. Shortly thereafter the team was invited to present their results at a seminar for Sir Ron – and this was done on 22 September 1993. The seminar presentation was structured to address the 'themes' of the Dearing review (see below). While these might be considered as distinct from the four-part model used to synthesise results in the report (Figure 2.2), the team was not unaware of the concerns as many of these emerged during the two-year period of the project and as such were addressed at least in part in the syntheses presented in the previous section in this chapter.

The Dearing review of the NC – Recommendations from the Mathematics Evaluation Project at KS 1, 2 and 3

The Recommendations from the project were regrouped/presented to correspond to the areas specified in the (Dearing) review. (NB: The numbers given with the Recommendations below correspond to those in the project Final Report, pages 237–38, and Summary Report, pages 29–30; Askew *et al.*, 1993.)

Theme: scope for slimming down the curriculum (mathematics)

Recommendation 1: Retain the statutory mathematics Order in place, without any slimming down, until teachers of all year groups have had a sufficiently long period working with it fully to articulate its strengths and weaknesses. For assessment and reporting purposes at KS1 and 2, merge the contents of some ATs with others at Levels 1–4 or 1–5.

Theme: the 10-level scale

Recommendation 2: Retain the 10-level scale, at least for the foreseeable future until an alternative is found that is demonstrably preferable.

Theme: assessment arrangements

Recommendation 5: In co-ordination with teachers and other interested groups, exercise close scrutiny of the national tests, ensuring that over several years they take as broad as possible a view of the SoAs, and incorporate different aspects of them. This will avoid the meanings of the SoAs becoming narrow, limited and readily coachable.

Recommendation 6: Ensure in the assessment Order for each key stage that the forms of assessment contain as much breadth as possible, including differentiation by outcome, and that at least in some parts of the tests, assessment of Ma1 is integrated with that of other ATs.

Recommendation 10: Place a high priority on teacher assessment, both as a formative process and as contributing to a summative result. Carry out further research in schools to determine what level of formative assessment is feasible and desirable, and use this to provide further guidance to teachers.

Theme: time and process

Recommendation 3: Allocate a period for extensive development, trialling and evaluation for any proposed changes to the statutory Order, before they can pass into law.

Recommendation 11: Encourage structures for professional development, especially in relation to teachers' subject knowledge and curriculum planning.

This requires linking with the Department for Education (DFE), HE, LEAs and other agencies to ensure that time and provision within Initial Teacher Training (ITT) are adequate, and that ITT is seen as only the first step in a continuing programme of professional development. This includes ensuring that Inset, such as the present 20-day courses, and also extended provision for secondary teachers, are increased. The involvement of teachers in research in association with HE institutions should be encouraged. Financial resources must be available to teachers for personal, as well as institutional, professional development, and must be used for this purpose.

Recommendation 14: Provide advice and guidance to publishers on the intentions and requirements of the Order, and on future developments. Provide publishers with a plan for review covering a period of 10 years, which will be maintained, so as to enable them to plan the preparation of new materials. Give sufficient notice between any changes to the Order and their implementation, so that materials can be designed, written and trialled.

Recommendation 16: Continue to use existing and strengthened links with professional associations, LEAs, Ofsted and HE to consult and monitor opinion, and to use their networks for dissemination and support.

Recommendation 17: Continue to monitor implementation of the NC carefully, and to take action in consultation with the profession to correct discernible ill-effects, including authorising research where necessary, possibly in association with other bodies.

Theme: support for teachers

Recommendation 4: Start as soon as possible to work with groups of teachers to design and trial a key-staged document to form a basis for teachers' planning, relating to current SoAs. This would start as a non-statutory document, with the likelihood of parts of it becoming a new statutory programme of study after appropriate and rigorous trialling.

Recommendation 7: Assist teachers to interpret SoAs by providing guidance other than that of test items. This should be in the form of exemplar classroom material, including pupils' work, some of which integrates Ma1 with other ATs. This would also provide guidance for publishers, and for the teams writing the tests.

Recommendation 8: Award priority to using and applying mathematics (Ma1) for the provision of support to teachers. Support should include extensive extended Inset, further exemplar materials, advice to publishers and stimulus for in-school reflection and development. Consider commissioning work to study and report on successful collaborative whole-school planning relating to UAM (Ma1).

Recommendation 9: Encourage more resources in terms of cover and/or advisory support to be given to schools for whole-school or departmental planning of schemes of work in mathematics, and development and/or selection of learning activities.

Recommendation 12: Prepare explanatory documents for parents and employers which address the philosophy and goals for each of the curriculum subjects. In the case of mathematics this will include the broad but holistic nature of the subject and the variety of teaching/learning experiences likely to be used in schools to develop competence. It will include advice relating to the benefits of informed and critical use of commercial schemes.

Recommendation 13: Give attention to policy for IT use and development at all levels, school, LEA and national, which includes providing additional guidance to teachers, increasing the level of support provided by advisory staff both within and across schools and increasing the provision of IT resources, enabling easy access by pupils and teachers.

Recommendation 15: Encourage reversal of the present trend of decrease in resource provision for mathematics advisory and support staff, at school, LEA and national levels, and in HE.

POLICY AND POLITICS

The degree to which the above influenced the policy and practice of the government and governmental agencies will be returned to in Chapter 6. Before attempting to link the discussions in Chapters 1 and 2 with the final chapter, selected outcomes from the research are elaborated on in the following chapters – Chapter 3 addresses issues associated with the use of commercial schemes, Chapter 4 that of teachers' professional development in working on aspects of sequencing and progression in the Order, and Chapter 5 the 'reading of the text' for Ma1 – teachers' interpretations of the meaning behind the rhetoric.

3

SOLVING TEACHERS' PROBLEMS? THE ROLE OF THE COMMERCIAL MATHEMATICS SCHEME

Alison Millett and David C. Johnson
King's College London

This chapter looks at two of the themes investigated by the evaluation of the implementation of NC mathematics – planning and difficulties. It takes one of the major findings of the planning study – that the use of commercial mathematics schemes is a major factor in teachers' planning – and suggests that some difficulties in implementation identified in the second area of study might be exacerbated rather than resolved by over-reliance on schemes.

BACKGROUND

Planning

At the end of the first year of the implementation of the NC, the NCC was reporting that the likelihood of mathematics involving the continued use of a commercial scheme was 'the most distinctive aspect of the implementation of the mathematics Order' at KS1 (NCC, 1991, p. 52). Most case-study schools consulted by the NCC were using commercial schemes in Yr1, and the need for extensions to commercial schemes was frequently reported. The mathematics Order was being used to map commercial mathematics schemes to NC requirements. At KS3 widespread use of commercial schemes was reflected in less use of the mathematics Order than of other subject Orders, for example science.

The planning task was seen as one of reviewing the existing published scheme to see how well it matched with the NC, rather than using the Order to plan new schemes of work. KS3 teachers were also making more use of ATs rather than PoS, even when they were not using commercial schemes.

HMI reporting in the same year also pointed to 'too limited a concentration when planning on statements of attainment and ATs, rather than using them as targets set in a broader mathematics curriculum', and that this 'compounded the fragmentation experienced by pupils' (HMI, 1991a, p. 15). They also noted the slow development of schemes of work.

These concerns noted by NCC and HMI led to the identification of planning as one of the issues to be addressed by the second stage of monitoring, and the request for an evaluation of the effectiveness of the PoS as a basis for in-school planning and their relationship in practice with SoAs.

Many different factors were seen to affect the planning of the implementation of the mathematics NC, and any attempt to understand the use made by teachers of the PoS would, of necessity, also include consideration of the use of commercial schemes, the degree of cross-curricular planning, the involvement of teachers in collaborative planning, and the extent to which teachers were differentiating curricula, as well as a more straightforward consideration of the extent and type of NC document use.

Concern about over-reliance on commercial schemes continued. In 1992 HMI noted that commercial mathematics schemes continued to be the dominant influence on the work being done in each key stage in mathematics, and that this removed the need, according to many teachers, for the school to undertake detailed planning of the curriculum (HMI, 1992a).

Ofsted, reporting more recently on the teaching and learning of number in primary schools (1993b, p. 16), indicated that

> In over a third of classes there was an over-reliance upon a particular published scheme which usually led to pupils spending prolonged periods of time in which they worked at a slow pace, often on repetitive, undemanding exercises, which did little to advance their skills or understanding of number, much less their interest and enthusiasm for mathematics.

The focus of these comments was on the way the schemes were used, and the extent of their use, rather than on the schemes themselves. Indeed, Ofsted reported that '[there were] many examples of good number work based upon published mathematics schemes, but such work was almost always supplemented by other materials in the form of work cards and practical tasks designed by teachers in the school' (*ibid.*, p. 15).

In 1992 HMI estimated that 99 per cent of schools used a published scheme for Yr2 and 3 pupils and two-thirds of the middle and secondary schools used them for Yr7 and 8 pupils (HMI, 1992a). However these figures tell us little about the extent of use within these schools and whether or not the schemes provided the major part of the pupils' mathematics. Nor do they in any way differentiate between schemes. These published schemes are no more homogeneous a group than the teachers who make use of them.

Published schemes in Britain vary considerably in the way in which the mathematics content is organised, the provision made for progression and differentiation, the integration of UAM (Ma1) with the rest of the mathematics curriculum, and the suitability of the work for a variety of teaching styles. Publishers of some schemes suggest that the use of their materials is all that is needed to ensure the implementation and 'coverage' of the NC. Others provide advice to teachers for extending activities and thereby perhaps developing their own materials to provide elements to support, say, differentiation or collaborative learning environments. However, the intentions of those who write the schemes may not be transferred to the teachers who use them; the way in which schemes are used by individual teachers, as well as the extent of their use, may not reflect these intentions. Bauersfeld (1979, p. 204) distinguishes among the intended, implemented and achieved curricula, describing them as 'the matter meant', 'the matter taught' and 'the matter learned'.

Difficulties

Within the theme of 'difficulties', the evaluation project was asked to identify the reasons for implementation difficulty (e.g. lack of clarity in the Order, lack of teacher knowledge and understanding of mathematics, conceptual difficulty for pupils, etc.) and recommend courses of action for remedying the problem. The areas of shape and space, algebra and handling data (including probability) had been identified as causing particular difficulty.

After the project team started work in September 1991, there was an additional report from HMI on the second year of the implementation of mathematics in the ERA (HMI, 1992a). This report noted that, although progress had been made in filling content gaps, work remained to be done at KS1 and 2 in relation to algebra, shape and space, and handling data and selected aspects of number work such as approximation and estimation. They also reported that the important area of UAM was underdeveloped. At KS3, HMI found that schools continued to fill content gaps, although aspects of number/algebra and handling data and probability were still not fully resolved. They identified the major issue remaining as that of UAM. However, the connections between content gaps or lack of coverage and difficulties were not spelt out in this monitoring.

SELECTED ANALYSES AND RESULTS – PLANNING

At an early stage in the questionnaire analysis it became apparent that the type and extent of use of commercially produced materials played a major role in decisions made by teachers about planning.

Mathematics advisers in the groups consulted for the project were aware of the major role played by schemes in the implementation of the mathematics NC. Schools at all key stages were using schemes in the areas in which these advisers worked, with one group of advisers noting a slight move away from scheme use, another group indicating that scheme use was about the same, and two groups feeling that the NC had pushed schools back towards schemes at KS1 and 2. (Comments from publishers also reinforced this last view.) There were feelings that the purchase of a scheme was now a top priority for reasons of security and pressure of time. There were also indications that some schools at KS3 were coming to realise that their dependency on the commercial scheme would need to be reduced and that some alternative, e.g. planning in terms of some modularisation of the mathematics curriculum, might be the way forward.

Findings from questionnaire data

Question 15 in the questionnaire (see Appendix 1 for full questionnaire) provided information on teachers' estimates of the proportion of pupils' mathematics work which was from a commercial scheme. They were asked to indicate which of six categories best described their practice (see Table 3.1). For teachers in all key stages the modal use of scheme was 51–80 per cent, but differences between key stages were apparent. The use of schemes increased through the key stages from KS1 to 3, with 33 per cent of KS1 teachers, 59 per cent of KS2 teachers and 79 per cent of KS3 teachers reporting pupils using a commercial scheme for more than 50 per cent of their work.

For the purposes of this chapter, teachers who used a scheme for more than 50 per cent of the pupils' work have been categorised as 'high scheme users'. 'Medium scheme users' are defined here as those classes in which pupils used a scheme for 21–50 per cent of their mathematics (see Table 3.1). The remaining teachers, designated as 'low or non-scheme users,' were predominantly teaching in KS1, with 45 per cent of the respondents saying that pupils used a scheme for no more than 20 per cent of their mathematics work (only 17 per cent of KS2 teachers and 13 per cent of KS3 teachers came into this category). Note that it was also the case that 11 per cent of KS1 teachers indicated that they did not use a scheme at all – substantially different from the percentages of teachers at KS2 and 3 in this category.

Table 3.1 Proportion of pupils' mathematics work done from a commercial scheme (question 15) (%)

	n	0	1–5	6–20	21–50	51–80	>80
KS1	215	11	15	19	23	27	6
KS2	282	4	6	7	24	49	10
KS3	237	4	4	5	8	41	38

Table 3.2   Frequency of use of (selected) documents in planning (question 5) (%)

	n	Yearly	Termly	Half-termly	Weekly	Daily	Never
NC document	707	7	19	43	25	4	2
LEA material	518	17	16	16	4	1	47
HMI material	488	21	9	7	1	0	62
Teachers' handbooks (comm. schemes)	659	3	6	20	40	25	6
Students' books (comm. schemes)	584	2	3	11	38	35	10
Materials developed in school	618	2	8	22	34	27	7
Magazines and periodicals	524	8	19	35	8	2	29

Note: Percentages given are of teachers (across all key stages) who responded to each part of the question. It should be noted that the number of respondents answering each part of the question differed.

If a scheme was being used to the extent outlined above for pupils in the three key stages, then it was likely that scheme materials were being used for planning mathematics work. This proved to be the case. Question 5 in the questionnaire asked teachers to indicate the frequency of use of different documents in their planning. As indicated in Table 3.2, teachers' handbooks and students' books from schemes formed an important part of the materials used by teachers in their planning and, when used, they were used frequently.

More teachers indicated that they used NC documents for planning than any other documents specified. However, of those who used NC documents, modal use was half-termly (43 per cent), with 29 per cent using them weekly or daily. Of those who used handbooks from a scheme, modal use was weekly, with 65 per cent using them weekly or daily. Fewer teachers used students' books for planning (584 vs. 659), but of those who did, modal use was again weekly, with 73 per cent using them weekly or daily. The only other category of materials which many teachers used was that of 'materials developed in school'. In this category, modal use was weekly, with 61 per cent using them weekly or daily. Where teachers were using teachers' handbooks and students' books for their planning they used them more frequently than other materials.

Findings from interview data – use of schemes

Confirmation of the importance of schemes in the planning process became evident in the early stages of interviewing, and analysis of the interview data reinforced this impression. When teachers were asked in interview to describe some mathematics that they had been doing in their classroom as a precursor to describing the planning for that mathematics, their descriptions almost invariably included reference to some mathematics from a scheme, as did their subsequent descriptions of the planning which led up to those activities.

The coding scheme derived from and used in the analysis of the interview data yielded three levels for describing the type and extent of scheme use in planning; these were denoted as *scheme-driven* planners, *scheme-assisted* planners and *low-scheme* planners.

Scheme-driven *planners*

Of the 11 interview teachers identified as *scheme-driven* (all of whom were from KS2 and 3), the scheme was clearly the starting point for their planning. High scheme use seemed to be associated with low NC document use and, at KS2, a limited amount of cross-curricular work. At KS3 high scheme use was associated with low or medium NC document use and low percentages of work related to UAM. The one teacher who categorised his use of UAM as high felt that it was all being addressed through the scheme and included practical work and real-life problems as well as investigations. All but one of the *scheme-driven* teachers indicated that they used a scheme for more than 80 per cent of the mathematics work they did with their class. A variety of different schemes was used and pupils in the classroom of a *scheme-driven* planner would be likely to be working individually through scheme books or cards.

Of the four KS2 teachers, three were using the NC documents for checking coverage, with one using them for planning. None of the KS3 teachers seemed to be using the documents on an ongoing basis for planning purposes.

Scheme-assisted *planners*

This was a more disparate group in that while they made moderate or considerable use of a scheme on the whole, they differed from the *scheme-driven* group in that it was not the first avenue of their planning. These teachers used the scheme (often very frequently) to fill what they saw were their needs and the needs of the pupils in their class, and they identified these needs through a consideration of other documents. The primary teachers made slightly more use of cross-curricular work, but perhaps the most salient difference between this group and the *scheme-driven* teachers was in the greater use of the NC documents for planning.

The group of *scheme-assisted* planners consisted of three KS1 teachers, six KS2 teachers and two KS3 teachers. Of the primary teachers, seven of the nine used a scheme with their class for more than 50 per cent of the time (high scheme users), one for 21–50 per cent (medium scheme user) and one for 20 per cent (low scheme user). The group made more use of NC documents than the *scheme-driven* group. Four of the primary teachers were high document users, with three of these using both PoSs and SoAs, three were medium document users (the modal group for KS1 and two teachers from questionnaire data), and one was a low document user. Teachers in this group were using the NC documents for planning (eight/nine) and for check-ing coverage (eight/nine). The primary teachers in this group also made more use of cross-curricular work than those in the *scheme-driven* group. Seven of the nine were using cross-curricular topics as a planning vehicle to a limited extent.

Of the two KS3 teachers in the *scheme-assisted* group, one was a high scheme and high document user, and one a medium scheme and medium document user. Both used the documents for planning and checking. One of these teachers regarded the amount of work involving UAM as high and consisting mainly of practical work and real-life problems, and one as low and consisting of investigations, real-life problems and practical work.

The schemes appeared to be used both for individualised work and for group work, and sometimes in both ways by certain teachers. There were some indications that number work was more likely to be conducted in an individ-ualised, ongoing way.

Low-scheme *planners*

These teachers used a scheme (or schemes) for less than 20 per cent of their work (often to a very limited extent) and on the whole selected from a variety of resource materials. They used a school/departmental scheme of work, their own scheme of work, the NC documents or a combination of these in their planning. Teachers in the *low-scheme* group tended to be high or medium NC document users, with the primary teachers characterised by the use of a cross-curricular topic as a vehicle for some of their planning.

This group contained more KS1 teachers than the other two groups and consisted of six KS1 teachers, one KS2 teacher and one KS3 teacher. The modal document use for this group was half-termly (medium document use), with two KS1 teachers and one KS3 teacher reporting high document use and one KS1 teacher reporting low document use. There was considerable use of the documents for planning (seven/eight) with five out of the seven primary teachers using them for checking coverage. The KS3 teacher defined her use of UAM as low, but considered that she included investigations, practical work and real-life problems within this.

Scheme-assisted and *low-scheme* planners generally used the scheme as one of a range of resources, and defined their needs with the help of this range – the diversity in approaches of *scheme-assisted* planners in particular indicating that it was possible to combine high-scheme use with frequent use of NC documents and other resources such as school or individual schemes of work. Pupils in the classrooms of *scheme-assisted* or *low-scheme* planners would be likely to be working in attainment groups on pages or exercises selected from the scheme by the teacher, or on work which the teachers had themselves prepared. Some pupils might be working in an individualised way through selected sections of the scheme.

Table 3.3 Contrasting interview sample with full questionnaire sample on data cross-tabulations

Teacher type	Key stage		High doc./ high scheme	Med. doc./ high scheme	Low doc./ high scheme	Med. doc./ med. scheme	High doc./ low scheme	Med. doc./ low scheme	Low doc./ low scheme
Scheme-driven	KS2	Interview (4)			4/4				
		Questionnaire			13%				
	KS3	Interview (7)		3/7	4/7				
		Questionnaire		22%	34%				
Scheme-assisted	KS1	Interview (3)	1/3		1/3			1/3	
		Questionnaire	7%		10%			27%	
	KS2	Interview (6)	3/6	1/6	1/6	1/6			
		Questionnaire	18%	24%	13%	11%			
	KS3	Interview (2)	1/2			1/2			
		Questionnaire	15%			1%			
Low-scheme	KS1	Interview (6)					2/6	3/6	1/6
		Questionnaire					12%	27%	5%
	KS2	Interview (1)						1/1	
		Questionnaire						7%	
	KS3	Interview (1)					1/1		
		Questionnaire					5%		

Contrasting interview and questionnaire data

When the interview sample was contrasted with the full questionnaire sample (see Table 3.3), the data suggested that it was likely that considerable numbers of KS3 teachers in particular shared some of the characteristics of the *scheme-driven* teachers who were interviewed, with 56 per cent of KS3 teachers falling into the two categories occupied by *scheme-driven* planners. At KS2, 13 per cent of the questionnaire sample shared the characteristics of scheme and document use with the interviewees categorised as *scheme-driven*.

SELECTED ANALYSES AND RESULTS – DIFFICULTIES

Findings from questionnaire data

As has already been mentioned, NCC and HMI monitoring did not spell out the difference between difficulties and lack of coverage. Responses to question 33 on the questionnaire revealed that in several areas of mathematics, and for several ATs in particular, teachers felt that their coverage was not yet adequate (see Table 3.4). When these responses were cross-tabulated with responses to the full range of difficulties, it was clear that, in some cases, there was some salient association between difficulty and inadequate coverage.

Full details of the areas of difficulty identified by this research project, and teachers' perceived reasons for these difficulties, can be found in the main report (Askew *et al.*, 1993). A summary of the reasons for difficulties identified by at least 10 per cent of KS1, 2 and 3 teachers is given in Table 3.5. The focus in the discussion here will be on those where the commercial mathematics scheme was seen to play an important role.

Teachers' perceptions were that their difficulties lay mainly in three areas: those of UAM (Ma1), handling data (Ma5) and algebra (Ma3). When they were asked to identify reasons for these difficulties, both questionnaire and interview data indicated several reasons which related closely to scheme use. Lack of availability of resources was given as a reason for difficulties; at all key stages teachers felt that they lacked suitable activities in probability, and that

Table 3.4 ATs not adequately covered (question 33)

	UAM		Number				Meas.	Algebra			Shape & space		Handling data		Prob.
AT	1	9	2	3	4	8	5	6	7	10	11	12	13	14	
KS1	11%	15%	3%	10%	17%	12%	7%	43%	49%	8%	35%	15%	17%	46%	
KS2	13%	15%	0%	2%	10%	7%	11%	38%	48%	8%	37%	18%	15%	51%	
KS3	20%	30%	0%	1%	6%	9%	6%	22%	23%	10%	25%	21%	21%	42%	

Note: Context for the question was set to be the teacher's own experience in the preceding year.

Table 3.5 All key stages: which of the following difficulties do you feel would apply to the areas of mathematics given? (question 36)

	UAM	Num.	Meas.	Alg.	Shape & space	Hand. data	Prob.
Lack of previous experience of teaching this area of the curriculum	1 2 3			1 2		1 2 3	1 2 3
Lack of availability of suitable activities	2 3			1 2		2 3	1 2 3
SoAs or PoS too difficult for pupils taught				1 2 3			1 2 3
Not easy to integrate into topic work				1 2 3			1 2
Not well covered by commercial scheme	1 2 3			2	2	1 2 3	1 2 3
Lack of clarity in the meaning of SoAs or PoS	1 2 3			2		2	2
Lack of confidence in own knowledge of area	2			2		1 2	1 2
Inadequate teaching material	2 3		1 2	2	2 3	1 2 3	1 2 3
Classroom management and organisation a problem	1 3		2			2 3	
Inadequate equipment	3		1 2 3		2 3	2 3	1 2 3
Requires change in teaching style	1 2 3						
Difficulties in making provision for different levels of attainment	1 2 3	2	2	2 3	2	1 2 3	1 2 3
Sequencing of SoAs problematic	3	3	3	3	3		3
Too much to get through	1 2 3	1 2 3	1 2 3	1 2 3	1 2 3	1 2 3	1 2 3
	UAM	Num.	Meas.	Alg.	Shape & space	Hand. data	Prob.

Notes:
1. Difficulty for 10% or more of KS 1 teachers.
2. Difficulty for 10% or more of KS 2 teachers.
3. Difficulty for 10% or more of KS 3 teachers.

they had inadequate teaching materials in handling data (particularly probability). The areas of UAM, handling data and probability were mentioned most frequently as being not well covered by the commercial scheme. Difficulties with making provision for different levels of attainment were particularly evident at KS2, where all areas of mathematics were affected.

At all key stages and in all the areas of mathematics, teachers indicated that there was 'too much to get through'. The issue of the manageability of the delivery of the mathematics curriculum was clearly an important one. Percentages for 'too much to get through' ranged between 11 and 33 per cent depending on area of mathematics and key stage. In some areas of mathematics over one-third of the teachers who expressed the perception that there was 'too much to get through' had no other difficulties in that area of mathematics.

Key areas of difficulty for classroom management and organisation were UAM at KS1 and 3, handling data at KS2 and 3, and measures at KS2. Teachers at all three key stages felt that the implementation of UAM caused difficulties related to the need for a change in teaching style. Teachers were worried about their lack of subject knowledge and their lack of experience in teaching certain areas. Teachers at all three key stages felt that they lacked experience in teaching UAM, handling data and probability. KS1 and 2 teachers lacked confidence in their subject knowledge, particularly in handling data.

ISSUES EMERGING FROM THE DATA

Findings from the evaluation indicated that some teachers made extensive and sometimes uncritical use of a commercial mathematics scheme, and were using this scheme as a mediator of the NC. Questionnaire data suggested that a much larger group of teachers, particularly at KS3, shared some characteristics of scheme and document use with these teachers. The evaluation also noted areas of difficulty for teachers which related to scheme use. Not all the _scheme-driven_ teachers (interviewed) maintained an uncritical approach to their commercial scheme on the issues which follow, nor did they necessarily report the difficulties described. It is noted here that these issues emerged from a general consideration of the data, not merely from interviews with those categorised as _scheme-driven_, but in several cases from those where _scheme-assisted_ or _low-scheme_ planners described their more circumspect use of scheme materials. However, _scheme-driven_ planners did use a narrower range of resources than both _scheme-assisted_ and _low-scheme_ planners.

It will of course have been noticed, not least by those involved in the preparation of commercial schemes, that all schemes appear to have been 'tarred with the same brush', by being discussed together. It is fully recognised that some commercial schemes are designed to be 'all that the teacher needs' whereas others specifically place the teacher in the central role and insist that the scheme should be only a part of the mathematics work experienced by each child. There were indications from questionnaire data that some schemes were more likely to be used as core materials than others, which were more often used as one of a number of resources. However, whatever the intentions of the publishers, it is the use made by teachers of commercial materials which affects the mathematics experienced by pupils in the classroom.

Many teachers who use a commercial scheme for the great majority of the mathematics work in their classrooms may feel that the issues described below do not present serious problems for them; they are aware of some or even all the issues and have made provision for dealing with these in their teaching.

Difficulties with coverage

A concern about the provision of a broad and balanced mathematics curriculum has been expressed both by the NCC and HMI. Advisers consulted by the project felt that some schools relied on schemes to provide coverage and to address all issues, and in this regard when gaps were identified merely waited for new materials. Four groups of advisers noted that schools were looking to change their schemes, and reasons given included a realisation that their current schemes were not covering all mathematical areas adequately (notably at KS1 and 2), or were not delivering in areas of perceived difficulty, with UAM of particular concern.

Teachers interviewed fell into two distinct categories relating to the resources they relied on when planning for coverage of the curriculum. One group looked predominantly to their scheme to provide coverage, and identified any gaps through a matching exercise with the NC documents. For most of these teachers (by definition *scheme-driven*), the mathematics outside the scheme would consist of material which they prepared to fill these identified gaps. At KS3 this was mainly investigational work identified to aid in the implementation of UAM. Other documents, for example a school scheme of work, might be used in conjunction with the scheme to ensure coverage.

For *scheme-assisted* and *low-scheme* teachers, the focus was generally on the NC documents to ensure coverage of the four content ATs (number, algebra, shape and space, and data handling), with additional use of school schemes of work if they were available. This combination of documents was used both for the planning of cross-curricular work and for the planning of mathematics topics. These teachers used the variety of resources available to them to plan the work outside the scheme, and looked to the scheme to fill certain identified needs.

If considerable numbers of teachers relied on their scheme for coverage, the breadth and balance of the curriculum would depend on how well the scheme covered each of the different areas of mathematics. When teachers were asked in the questionnaire about difficulties they had found with scheme coverage of the mathematical topics, quite large percentages (particularly at KS2) reported

Table 3.6 Areas not well covered by the commercial scheme (question 36e) (%)

	UAM	Number	Measure.	Algebra	Shape & space	Handling data	Probability
KS1	15	1	9	7	8	23	35
KS2	22	1	5	24	10	29	49
KS3	22	0	2	4	5	23	15

that certain areas were 'not well covered by the commercial scheme' (see Table 3.6). (Difficulties were considered worthy of comment if they were identified as problematic by 10 per cent or more of the questionnaire respondents in a key stage.)

When any association with coverage was interrogated using cross-tabulations, it appeared that at KS1, 'not well covered' by the scheme was associated with inadequate coverage in the area of UAM. Of the 11 per cent of teachers who felt that their coverage of UAM was not adequate over the previous year, nearly one-half (5 per cent) also felt that UAM was not well covered by the scheme. At KS2 an association with scheme use extended to more areas of mathematics. Nearly one-half of the 51 per cent of KS2 teachers who felt that they were not covering probability adequately in the previous year also felt that this area was not well covered by the scheme. The proportions were about one-third for handling data. The major difficulties at KS3 were focused on handling data, where one-third of teachers who felt their coverage was inadequate also indicated that handling data was not covered well by the scheme, and UAM where the proportions were one-third or slightly over. The perception that certain areas were not well covered by the commercial scheme was associated with inadequate coverage of UAM at KS1, probability and handling data at KS2 and handling data and UAM at KS3.

Several teachers in the interviews mentioned that the schemes they were using did not cover well certain areas of mathematics. It seemed that 'not covering well' could relate to content or presentation, or both. There seemed to be a focus on certain areas, with UAM, handling data and probability being mentioned, as in the questionnaire data, but number, measures, and shape and space also being identified.

A Yr8 teacher, using a commercial scheme for over 80 per cent of work with the class: 'the SCHEME books themselves don't . . . take investigations much into account . . . so it's a case of us having to supplement that in year 8, and I don't think we've given them enough of a diet, if the truth be told, of investigations.' There were indications from some of the interviewees that the difficulty of some areas not being well covered by the scheme was being addressed by the publishers. A Yr9 teacher, not using a scheme with the pupils, but commenting on the use of a commercial scheme with Yr7 and 8:

Q: You've said that handling data and probability are not well covered by the commercial scheme.

A: No, they're not well covered in years 7 and 8 by the SCHEME. Since I filled this in [questionnaire] we've had some new booklets from SCHEME . . . particularly on handling data. So they [publishers] were aware of the gap as well.

Contact with publishers of mathematics materials indicated that they themselves had identified areas where supplementary materials were needed and these were being produced. Several entirely new schemes were in preparation but this was a lengthy process. The 'planning blight' on the production of new commercial schemes caused by changes to the NC Order in 1991 (DES/WO, 1991) and the subsequent announcement of a major review of all NC subjects (resulting in new Orders in 1995) meant unavoidable delay in the preparation of new materials, and although the consequent difficulties due to lack of materials were being addressed through the publication of supplementary material in many of the content areas, the lack of materials which support the view of UAM as a vehicle for the other main content areas still remained a source of concern. It was also suggested that financial constraints may have affected the ability of schools to purchase the most up-to-date materials.

Difficulties with UAM

As described previously, UAM was one of the areas which questionnaire respondents felt was 'not covered well' by their scheme. Teachers expressed other anxieties about this AT, feeling that a change of teaching style might be needed for its implementation. (Further documentation and justification for such a view is given in Chapter 5.)

Analysis of interview data relating to teachers' understanding of this AT established a wide variation in interpretation; some of these interpretations were very limited in scope, bearing in mind the breadth of intentions expressed in materials designed to provide supplementary support for this area, the NSG (DES/WO, 1989b).

The models of UAM presented by some commercial schemes may have reinforced a limited interpretation; in particular, the apparent assumption that any mention of the 'real world' must necessarily invoke this aspect of mathematics. Some commercial schemes produced separate booklets for activities incorporating UAM, in contrast to the expectation that it should be 'permeating the curriculum' as suggested in the NSG.

The presentation of problem-solving and investigational activities as extension work for the more able pupils which could be found in some schemes also gave rise to concern about entitlement for the less able to engage in work incorporating this AT.

Difficulties with differentiation

Ofsted, reporting on the third year of the implementation of the mathematics NC, drew attention to the ways in which schemes were used at both primary and secondary level. At KS1 and 2 they reported that 'rigid adherence to one scheme did not adequately meet the range of mathematical ability in the year group' (Ofsted, 1993c, p. 20). And at KS3, 'The best practice, in terms of providing well-matched work, with varied learning experiences and consistently good standards throughout, was in schools where a range of teaching materials was used' (*ibid.*, p. 21).

Ofsted also acknowledged the difficulty of matching the teaching to meet the different and developing abilities of pupils and noted further: 'While grouping by ability may not always be in the pupils' best interests, or can be accurately achieved, the alternatives, such as the over-reliance on individual work, often exacerbated by over-dependence on textbooks and worksheets which is evident in many schools, can present greater obstacles to progress' (*ibid.*, p. 38). Interview data from the evaluation project were able to provide some insights into ways in which different organisational practices were used by teachers, both within and outside the scheme.

Differentiation within the mathematics taken from a scheme seemed to be established either by having pupils working individually through scheme books or cards (the method favoured by the majority of *scheme-driven* planners), or by teacher intervention in selecting work from the scheme at the appropriate level, usually for attainment groups (the method favoured by the majority of *scheme-assisted* and *low-scheme* planners). The picture at KS3 was complicated by the organisational device of setting (ability grouping), practised by schools to which teachers in all these categories belonged. Six out of the 10 KS3 teachers interviewed reported setting for some classes in the school. In five of these six cases there was setting in classes which they were teaching, which provided the context for responding to both questionnaire and interview. Those working with pupils in setted classes sometimes had pupils working individually, or were either using different graded texts with different classes, or working at a different pace with different sets. All the KS3 interview teachers working with mixed-ability classes were using the strategy of individualised work.

As has already been stated, schemes varied one from another in the way in which they approached differentiation. All the publishers contacted for this project claimed to address differentiation in some way. This might be through 1) the provision of different booklets or programmes of booklets for different abilities; 2) core, development and extension sections suitable for different pupils; 3) tasks which could be addressed at different levels; and 4) variable outcomes enabled in investigational activities; or some combination of these. However, the role of the teacher in selecting appropriate activities or guiding pupils along appropriate paths was stressed in most cases. It was this intervention which appeared to be lacking in the approach of some interview teachers to the work that was done from the scheme, but it must be remembered that the design of some schemes where exercises on different areas of mathematics follow each other in swift succession did not easily lend itself to selection for individuals or groups.

Some interview teachers gave clear indications of intervention in the use of the scheme, with some KS3 teachers describing individualised programmes of work. Others (mainly at KS2) suggested that differentiation was by pace of working, with all pupils apparently working through the same exercises. A KS2 teacher (Yr3) described her dilemma on realising that working individually through the books did not necessarily address the levels at which pupils should be working:

> It's made me rethink what I do with them, and certainly I try now to . . . but you see, this is where the dilemma comes in . . . because if they work their way through all these SCHEME books . . . they don't get anywhere near the National Curriculum levels that are expected of them.

A scheme structure which consisted of different sections to address different pupils' needs within a framework of maths topics was to seen to be more successful by one *scheme-driven* teacher and indications about newer and future publications were that this approach to differentiation was being developed. There were also some indications that the extension work provided by the schemes was more likely to include investigational and open-ended activities for the more able, rather than for pupils of average or lower attainment, but again, this seemed to be an issue which was of concern to (and being addressed by) some publishers.

Difficulties with 'manageability'

The earlier quotation from the Yr3 teacher raised not only the issue of differentiation but also that of manageability – identified by teachers as a major concern. If children, by working their way through scheme books, are completing more exercises than they need (as Ofsted suggested was the case), then the amount of mathematics to be fitted into the time available will indeed become unmanageable. If teachers are not selecting only appropriate pages from scheme materials, but are allocating either whole sections of work or individualised work through the book, then it is quite possible that some children are completing more exercises than are necessary or valuable. (Other children may, of course, need more reinforcement than is in the scheme.) A Yr5 teacher, categorised as *scheme-assisted*, clearly illustrated his awareness of this problem, describing the importance he attached to remaining flexible about matching the repetition of examples to the needs of the child.

Difficulties with lack of experience or lack of subject knowledge

A lack of experience of teaching certain areas of mathematics was expressed as a difficulty by teachers at all key stages and a lack of subject knowledge by teachers at KS1 and 2. One group of advisers consulted for this project felt that the results of feelings of inadequacy over subject knowledge might well be an increased reliance on a commercial scheme. There were indications from interview data that this could be the case: 'Yes, when I first started teaching . . . I started off by using . . . not one particular scheme, but I used scheme books more, and it was only by getting more resources and talking to other teachers and building up a bank of resources . . . that I used them . . . less' (Yr6 teacher). This Yr6 teacher was able to move away from dependence on scheme materials as he built up his own resources; in his case this was with the support of attendance on a 20-day inservice course.

The research also indicated that collaborative work on the development of a school scheme of work (often the catalyst for the development of subject knowledge) was happening more frequently in schools where teachers were other than *scheme-driven*.

DISCUSSION

Mathematics has long been regarded by many teachers in Britain as a subject for which the textbook, or commercial scheme, is the main resource. Evidence from the IEA Second International Mathematics Study (Robitaille and Garden, 1989) indicates that this is a world-wide phenomenon. The IEA study sampled two populations of students, those in the grade where the majority of students had attained the age of 13/13+ years, and those in the normally accepted terminal grade of secondary education and who were studying mathematics as a substantial part of their academic programme. Questionnaires completed by teachers of these students revealed that textbooks containing both explanation and exercises were clearly a major resource, with published workbooks (exercises only) being used to a slightly lesser extent. In a comparison of school mathematics in Japan and the USA focusing on elementary and lower secondary schools, Miwa (1991, p. 413) noted that 'Both in Japan and the U.S., textbooks are valued as the main materials of teaching and learning in school education. Textbooks are important means of mediation between the intended curriculum and classroom practice, and we believe that textbooks reflect the teaching and learning style in each country'. Zhang (1991) noted there was a movement to place mathematics education reform on the national educational agenda in China, and that the process of reform was to be undertaken, at least in part, through the development of a new series of textbooks.

Over the past 30–40 years, large-scale curriculum development in the form of new sets of books has represented a major thrust in the attempts of many countries to change the mathematics being taught in schools, i.e. to implement 'modern' or 'new' mathematics. Criticisms of reliance on such an approach are not uncommon (e.g. see Burkhardt, Fraser and Ridgway, 1990). Johnson and Rising (1972) drew attention to the textbook as a major factor not only in determining what mathematical topics were taught and how they were taught but also in affecting the introduction of new topics into the curriculum. They described some of the dangers of textbook teaching where the focus was on the text rather than on the learner, and concluded that the textbook could be 'an invaluable servant or an intolerable master' (*ibid.*, p. 370).

Prior to the introduction of the mathematics NC in England and Wales (DES/WO, 1989a), the Cockcroft Report (1982, pp. 91–92), in discussing primary mathematics, warned:

> it is always necessary to use any textbook with discrimination, and selections should be made to suit the varying needs of different children. It may be better too, to tackle some parts of the work in an order which is different from that in the book or to omit certain sections for some or all children. It should not be expected that any textbook, however good, can provide a complete course to meet the needs of all children; additional activities of various kinds need to be provided.

Referring to the increased use of individualised commercial schemes for secondary mathematics, the same report indicated that

> In our view there are some major problems which need to be resolved when using such schemes. One is that of providing sufficient opportunities for oral work and discussion. Another is the difficulty of devising materials from which all pupils can learn satisfactorily and of ensuring that the necessary interconnections are established between the topic which is being studied and other pieces of mathematics.
>
> (*Ibid.*, p. 152)

In the light of the many concerns expressed, it is somewhat surprising that, while it is generally accepted that teacher's use and dependence on this medium is a common and potentially highly important phenomenon, the implications of this situation have had limited attention in mathematics education research (note Lerman, 1993, p. 71). This is not to say that selected aspects have not been addressed, e.g. social messages hidden in text material (Lerman, 1990); the uneven inclusion of 'new' material throughout the grades and notions of excessive repetitive practice (Flanders, 1987); or the influence of the textbook on students' attitudes (Grouws, Good and Dougherty, 1990), but rather that the phenomenon has not been investigated in any systematic way in regard to teachers', or pupils', perceptions and use.

The *scheme-driven* teachers identified earlier in this chapter indicated that the commercial scheme was their first avenue of planning. It is likely that this characteristic is shared by many teachers in the general population who are also high scheme users. These *scheme-driven* teachers seem to share some similarities with a group of teachers identified by Schmidt *et al.* (1987) in their study of 18 teachers of children in grades three to five in Michigan as 'classic textbook followers' for whom 'the textbook offers the primary definition of the content of instruction of mathematics: little else influences this type of teacher' (*ibid.*, p. 451). A second group of teachers, 'textbook follower/strong student influence', resembled the *scheme-assisted* group defined in this study, in that the textbook was the major source of content, but it was used to fit identified student needs and interest. It is interesting also that Schmidt and co-workers found that these two groups together accounted for two-thirds of their sample, as was the case with the teachers interviewed for this evaluation project in the UK.

Pressure to use a commercial scheme as the mainstay of their mathematics may be hard for teachers to withstand. This pressure is both internal and external. Internally it may stem from feelings of inadequacy about mathematics which afflict many primary teachers in particular, and in the present research, both publishers and advisers have noted that the requirements of the NC have in some cases added to these feelings of inadequacy. Anxieties about lack of experience or lack of subject knowledge might well be a reason for turning to commercial materials for support – a course of action which might not result in any development in the teacher's own knowledge or expertise in mathematics. In arguing for a more measured approach to scheme use, however, it should be noted that it may be the case that some teachers have little confidence in their mathematical or pedagogical content knowledge and hence a scheme would be of benefit both to them and to their pupils, and the teachers themselves are aware of this. Indeed it has been noted (Lockheed, Vail and Fuller, 1986) that the textbook can contribute to student learning in developing countries by substituting for deficiencies in post-secondary teacher education and by delivering a more comprehensive curriculum. Low scheme use may not necessarily be associated with good practice; it may sometimes be ideologically driven, leaving unconfident teachers presenting unbalanced and inadequate curriculum. Organisational, as well as epistemological, reasons for liking or using schemes or worksheets are also advanced by teachers (see, for example, Nias, Southworth and Campbell, 1992).

Externally, pressure may come from parents, from other teachers and from the children themselves. Many parents find it difficult to understand 'progression' that is not expressed through booklets completed or pages ticked off, and this in turn can lead to heavy pressure on a school to maintain or increase the amount of mathematics which comes from a commercial scheme. This may even extend to the provision of finances for the purchase of such a scheme.

Some teachers who do not feel that strict adherence to a scheme is in the best interests of their pupils may find themselves working in a school culture in which use of scheme is *de rigueur* and be unable to persuade their colleagues otherwise, even assuming they had the confidence to try.

Teachers interviewed for this research made many allusions to children's enjoyment when working from a commercial scheme, and Desforges and Cockburn (1987, p. 127) report that 'even when the teachers wanted to pause for thought, it seemed that the children could hardly wait to get back to their tables to "get on" with their cards'. The reasons for this apparent enthusiasm, interesting and important though they are, go beyond the scope of this chapter, except in terms of the pressure that this puts on the teacher. High scheme use may well have created an atmosphere in which scheme work has high status, and pupils come to regard it as 'proper mathematics'.

The pressures on teachers to use commercial schemes are only too evident. The function of this chapter has been to draw attention to several of the areas of implementation difficulty identified by teachers – areas where the use of a commercial scheme might be thought to solve these problems – and to point out that it is in just those areas that the drawbacks of over-reliance on schemes can become evident. Teachers will not necessarily solve their problems and may, in fact, exacerbate them by turning uncritically to commercial schemes.

In extreme cases of scheme reliance, pupils may neither be presented with activities which reflect their attainment nor with activities which adequately cover the breadth of the intended curriculum. They may never experience work incorporating UAM in the manner envisaged by the NSG, and regarded as essential for the development of skills of communication and reasoning in the application of mathematical knowledge and for developing an enjoyment of the subject itself (DES/WO, 1989b). The teachers may remain unfamiliar with the NC, and may never, as a result, achieve 'ownership' of it, and be able to internalise it and adapt it to their own use. There may be less co-operative work in a *scheme-driven* environment, with a consequent lack of development of subject knowledge. Finally, and perhaps most important of all to those teachers who are becoming demoralised in their struggle to implement the curriculum, they may not experience the enjoyment and professional satisfaction to be gained from knowing their pupils and planning the provision of activities appropriate to each pupil's mathematical development.

Until teachers can see the value of alternatives to the commercial schemes upon which they depend, there is not likely to be significant change in their use. The time needed to develop a scheme of work within a school which could be the basis of teachers' planning should not be underestimated, and maths co-ordinators and HoDs will need to have time set aside to facilitate such developments. Parents and governors will also need to be convinced of the value of teacher-designed and assessed activities, with at least equal value being given to these, as to completed pages of a book. The role of the NC in freeing teachers from textbooks by giving an alternative framework for planning has been realised and taken up enthusiastically by some teachers, and the benefits of working in this way could be made clearer to others.

No attempt has been made to broaden the scope of this chapter to include pupils' perceptions of the mathematics which they do from a commercial scheme. This aspect, important though it is, did not form part of the research, but would benefit from consideration in future research. Nor has the chapter attempted a critique of the view of mathematics presented by different schemes. There are many other issues related to the use of commercial schemes or textbooks which deserve attention; for example, the use of research evidence in the development of schemes and the possibilities of encouraging informed and critical use of schemes during teacher training.

One encouraging sign for the future is that some mathematics advisers are taking advantage of a situation where schools are looking to change their schemes, and in such a context developing a structured approach to looking critically at both existing and new schemes. This structured approach is helping schools to make an informed choice, as well as aiding in the identification of areas which require resources beyond the scheme selected. Such an approach provides opportunities for raising awareness not only of possible pitfalls and inadequacies but also of the positive features of well prepared and suitable commercial materials to be selected and used, with the teacher, rather than the scheme, in control of the mathematics presented to the pupils.

4

TEACHERS' PERCEPTIONS OF SEQUENCING AND PROGRESSION IN THE MATHEMATICS NATIONAL CURRICULUM

Stephanie Prestage
University of Birmingham

Progression is an attractive idea educationally; anybody who queries it is liable to look unreasonable.

(Barrs, 1994, p. 36)

This chapter has its foci in two areas – the professional development of the teachers as they participated in the activities of the two teacher groups along with the outcomes of their deliberations. Thus the story of professional development is imbedded in the account of the Mathematics Evaluation Project (Askew *et al.*, 1993) and it is the teachers' perceptions and recommendations as they addressed the tasks indicated in the specification which are highlighted here – to illustrate how their thinking evolved. My role in the evaluation was that of co-ordinator and member of one of the groups and this was extended for the purposes of this chapter to that of participant observer. The teachers' personal development and attempts to achieve 'ownership' of the curriculum over the two-year period became a fascinating story and provided further evidence of the importance of having an adequate period of time for trial, reflection and discussion.

INTRODUCTION

As indicated in Chapter 2, one of the tasks of the evaluation project was to consider the sequencing of statements and the definition of progression within the PoS and the ATs of the mathematics Order. Initially this was the 1989 Order, but in fact as draft documents were available for the 1991 Order it was this document which was used to guide the work. We were asked to address particularly the following:

- Whether SoAs were at the right level and consistent with one another.
- Whether there were gaps in the sequence of statements for some topics.
- Whether the implied developmental model for curriculum planning was consistent.

Two teacher groups were set up to support this study, one based in Cambridge and one in Birmingham. Each group comprised a co-ordinator from the research team and eight teachers from across the three key stages (KS1, 2 and 3). Working with teachers from across this range was particularly exciting as it enabled us to consider questions of progression across the age and attainment range. For example, was it possible to understand Level 4 in the mathematics Order regardless of age and maturity?

The teacher groups were formed through contact with the local mathematics inspectorate in each region. The Cambridge group consisted of the following:

Four teachers from a small rural LEA:

- two from first schools, both were teaching Yr2 classes,
- one from a primary school, teaching a Yr4 class, and
- one from a middle school, teaching a Yr5 class.

Four teachers from a rural LEA:

- two from primary schools, one teaching a reception class and one a combined Yr2 and 3 class, and
- two from middle schools, one teaching a Yr6 class and one a combined Yr7 and 8 class.

The Birmingham group consisted of the following:

Four teachers from a large inner-city LEA:

- two from secondary schools, both teaching across the 11–18 age range, and
- two from primary schools, one teaching a Yr2 class and one teaching a Yr4 class.

Four teachers from a smaller LEA:

- two from secondary schools, again both teaching across the age range, and
- two from primary schools, one teaching Yr5 and the other a Yr6 class.

The teacher groups met on 15 days over the two years. Given the fairly tight schedule and the brief for the project we decided to analyse each of the five ATs in turn and in the following order:

- Ma4 – space and shape.
- Ma3 – algebra.
- Ma5 – handling data including a separate focus on probability.
- Ma2 – number.
- Measures – the final meeting was spent looking at measures (from Ma2 and 4).

At each meeting evidence was gathered from

- examples of pupils' work (across the key stages) to consider the match between planning against the NC SoAs and PoS and pupil outcomes;
- discussions with colleagues in the teachers' own schools on perspectives of the NC, its interpretation and implementation; and
- identification of, and written reflection on, relevant aspects of the practice of all the teachers in the groups, followed by discussion and elaboration of issues that arose within the groups.

The teachers considered certain of the SoAs or aspects of the PoS which had been selected as a focus for discussion. This led to a consideration of

- meanings that could be attached to statements,
- expected levels of response from pupils,
- the development of progression through the levels,
- consistency within a level,
- the relationship of the PoS to the SoAs,
- the use of, and progression within, the strands, and
- the appropriateness and range of the examples given with the statements.

In addition evidence came from

- research literature and curriculum development reports that related to specific areas of mathematics and which offered some indications on sequencing and progression,
- SAT data where available, and
- project questionnaire and interview data (see Chapter 2 and Appendix 1).

Before discussing the work of the teacher groups and some of their conclusions, I would like to outline the history of the document that we were working with and consequently the model we were asked to analyse, followed by some general issues relating to sequencing and progression that arose over the two years.

THE ORDER

As noted in Chapter 1, a working group charged with defining a mathematics national curriculum was first established in August 1987. Their terms of reference were to define this curriculum with ATs and a related PoS. ATs were

defined as 'Clear objectives for the knowledge, skills, understanding and apti-
tudes which pupils of different abilities and maturity should be expected to
have acquired at or near certain ages', and a PoS as 'The essential content
which needs to be covered to enable pupils to reach or surpass the attainment
targets' (DES/WO, 1988, p. 1).

These targets were to be developed within the following framework described by the Secretary of State:

> By attainment targets I have in mind clearly specified objectives for what pupils
> should know, understand, and be able to do at or around the end of the academic
> year in which they reach the ages of 7, 11, 14 and 16 . . . I expect that the
> development of attainment targets and programmes of study will be an iterative
> process . . . I envisage that much of the assessment at 7, 11, and 14 will be school
> based. It will be done by teachers as an integral part of normal classroom work.
>
> *(Ibid.*, pp. 93–94)

The final report was published one year later. The working group defined 14
ATs. As to the levelling:

> We have found our task challenging and stimulating. The stimulus has come from
> knowing that we were breaking new ground in attempting to develop a mathe-
> matics curriculum with continuity and progression through from the primary re-
> ception class to the secondary fifth form. It would be surprising if we had got
> everything right first time . . . The only way this can be tested is empirically. It will
> be an important function of the National Curriculum Council (NCC) and of the
> Schools Examination and Assessment Council (SEAC) to advise on any necessary
> adjustments in the light of experience of these targets in use.
>
> *(Ibid.*, p. 1)

In describing the PoS the group decided that the content was present in the ATs
and there was no need for repetition:

> In describing the levels of attainment within the attainment targets that we have
> proposed . . . we have already described the content and skills and processes which
> pupils will need to cover in order to make progress within the attainment targets
> . . . In essence the targets determine what is taught and what is assessed, but they
> do not, on their own, specify a mathematics curriculum.
>
> *(Ibid.*, p. 63)

The working group's proposals included guidance as to how ATs should be
achieved. However, the published Order did not include this guidance but included instead a PoS (referred to in the proposals as a map of the curriculum)
which was a direct copy of the assessment statements – the repetition that the
working group had agreed there was no need to offer. The working group had
determined criteria for all pupils which was, according to their brief, to be mainly
teacher assessed. (Criterion referencing had been attempted some years earlier for
GCSE without success for the given assessment style, the external examination.
Existing models for criterion-referenced curriculum, e.g. the Structured

Mathematics Individualised Learning Experiment (SMILE) developed by teachers in ILEA and the GAIM Project (Brown, 1992a), are based mainly upon teacher assessment.) It was not surprising therefore that within their prescription for the curriculum are statements of varying conceptual demand within each level, statements which describe knowledge, skills and understanding, statements which might be covered in two weeks or even two years. For example, work on place value appears alongside understanding halves and quarters, work involving a database alongside mental arithmetic and estimation. The ATs, while intended to cover the whole curriculum, were a selection of the mathematics not an exhaustive list. In regard to external assessment, the working group suggested that 'since SATs are to be used to help moderate the teacher assessments . . . they should sample a broad and balanced range of attainment targets . . . a third of the statements' (DES/WO, 1988, p. 78).

The empirical testing did not happen. The need for change was determined by a new Secretary of State for Education and, within two years, another Order was in place. This new version (DES/WO, 1991) retained the PoS (the old assessment statements), halved the number of SoAs and reduced the number of ATs from 14 to 5. Some SoAs were retained, some excluded and some new ones written. Essentially the curriculum originally designed by the working group, the old model, was retained. As before, the assessment structure contained a variety of statements that might take a pupil two weeks or two years to attain and that demanded a range of activity – e.g. 3-D constructions, doing statistical surveys and using a computer. Reasons for the rewrite and for the choice of statements retained or excluded from the assessment structure were not made available, it 'just seemed to happen'.

A further significant change was brought about at this time – the move to external assessment of the curriculum through, for the most part, paper-and-pencil tests at the end of each key stage. Additionally these tests were to assess the majority of the SoAs – at KS2 and 3 across all five ATs, at KS1 a subset of the ATs. These results would also over-ride teacher assessments and league tables produced for comparing external assessment results between schools.

It is important to place the work of the project in the context of the time since we all arrived at the project with our own particular experiences. At the start of the project in September 1991 the study was faced with the dilemma of two versions of the NC in place. The teachers involved had experience of the 1989 Order with a mixture of teacher and external assessment. During the first year of the evaluation study they had to move to working with the 1991 Order and timed written tests at the end of each key stage – along with the introduction of policy which included published league tables and Ofsted inspections. Such changes influenced many of our discussions and the problems and solutions relating to the consistency of progression within the model shifted depending on our focus. For example, as we considered a PoS for teaching we sometimes found that we needed to go beyond our brief and consider the assessment structure for externally produced timed written tests.

GENERAL ISSUES

A number of issues emerged over the two years that had significance beyond that of an individual AT or all the targets. Concerns about the various parts of the defined curriculum and their relationship to each other as well as their sequencing and progression were raised in discussions. These issues grew out of the work on 'gaps', 'difficulties' and sequencing which had been the initial focus. The teachers felt that a consideration of these issues was as important to the evaluation of the implementation of the curriculum as the work on individual targets and was crucial to an understanding of progression in mathematics.

The mathematics curriculum as discrete areas

Many of the teachers in the group indicated that a common approach to organising the curriculum in their schools was to plan and deliver the mathematics through sequences within each of the separate ATs. Thus mathematics was made up of four or possibly five discrete areas. Though planning decisions were not determined by the documents, nevertheless, such an approach was fairly common – indeed it was such an approach that we had taken in our initial work. It was likely that the presentation of the mathematics in the NC documents encouraged this and the teachers claimed that it enabled them to account more easily to others for having covered all the curriculum. Concerns with accountability seemed to be initially more important than the mathematics itself and the group admitted that this could result in a narrowing of both the mathematical experiences encountered by pupils and of the pedagogic approaches adopted. Similar tensions were to be found in the interview data collected during the first year of the Mathematics Evaluation Project:

> the first thing that goes by the board is practical work, because it takes a long time. I mean you've got the time of taking the stuff out of the box and setting it up . . . and organising groups and stuff, and . . . [the teacher goes on to say what she thinks about this change] it's terrible. I mean maths is a hands-on activity.
>
> (Yr5 teacher)

Breadth and balance across the ATs

The teachers also suggested that problems would arise as a consequence of the content in some of the ATs being more dense than in others. For example, the number target was thought to be 'very full' and might lead to an overemphasis on number leading to difficulties in providing breadth and balance across all the targets; as one teacher commented, there was 'too great an emphasis on number and little real concern for aspects of shape and space and handling

Table 4.1 Percentages of teachers who responded that the AT had been 'covered well' (question 33)

	UAM		Number & Measures				Algebra			Space & shape		Handling Data		
1989 AT	1	9	2	3	4	8	5	6	7	10	11	12	13	14
KS1	62	49	90	69	38	51	60	13	20	56	23	33	33	12
KS2	52	42	84	84	45	55	34	17	15	57	25	39	39	11
KS3	37	27	84	83	57	47	52	42	42	51	37	35	40	24

data'. In addition it was felt that even within number the practice of calculation received the greater proportion of time and other aspects such as developing number concepts and estimation were not being properly considered: 'that's estimate and measure quantities and appreciate the approximate nature of measurement . . . so I think that's . . . it's a concept that's not taught particularly, and also it's probably one that we as maths teachers discourage' (comment from a KS3 teacher).

The teacher groups' concerns and the teacher comments were supported to a large extent by the questionnaire data (see Table 4.1). Question 33 of the questionnaire asked the teachers to say which of the ATs they covered well in their curriculum planning. The table shows the percentage of teachers saying that they 'covered well' each of the 14 ATs within the 1989 Order.

Teacher questionnaire responses indicated that number AT2 and 3 received much greater coverage than AT4, estimation and approximation. An emphasis on only certain aspects of number was also commented upon by Ofsted (1993b, p. 3): 'fewer than half the schools had schemes that offered guidance on the teaching of number; very few schemes paid sufficient attention to estimation and approximation or to the development of concepts in general.' The questionnaire percentages for shape and space and handling data indicated only limited coverage of these aspects of mathematics. Whether or not each of the ATs should be given equal weight in terms of teaching time was a question not explored in the questionnaire. The teacher groups raised questions about expectations from the curriculum, i.e. as there are now five ATs should they each receive the same time and attention or may teachers choose on the basis of what they deem to be appropriate for their pupils?

Too much to get through

Discussions about coverage soon led on to discussion of the belief that there was too much to get through, as one primary teacher commented: 'there is a definite overload in the number curriculum, and, there is a vast difference between "know" and "use".' (The teacher here was referring to SoAs such as the following, taken from the number curriculum (Ma2): 'Demonstrate that they know and can use number facts, including addition and subtraction.')

This comment was only one of many which related to recognition by the teacher groups and their colleagues of the developmental aspects of pupils' learning in mathematics. Their concerns were twofold. First, that combining words such as 'know' and 'use' in SoAs at the same level when dealing with number concepts gives the impression that one should know and use concurrently. Yet to attain knowledge and use of a numerical idea requires progression through a range of sequenced stages and opportunities to work with the numerical idea in a range of contexts. This takes a great deal of teaching time. Secondly, the number target (Ma2) was packed with similar statements which, as presented in the document, gave no indication of the developmental learning process involved. Hence giving due time to each aspect was proving difficult. This was supported by a comment from a reception teacher who, when provoked by a Level 1 statement from the number PoS – read, write and order numbers to 10 – said: 'Do they know how much work is involved in that?'

This teacher was expressing the frustrations of many. Obviously no one has denied the amount of work implied in this statement or other similar statements, but their brevity and perhaps terseness was seen (potentially) to produce adverse effects in terms of teacher attitudes and quality of teaching and outside pressures due to others' perceptions of the time needed to cover the content.

Progress in number dictating the level in mathematics for a pupil

Some concern was expressed that the document was causing teachers, for ease of working, to decide on a level in mathematics for pupils rather than an appropriate level in each target. This often led to the result that progress in number determined the teaching level across all ATs. It was felt that this might limit the complexity of challenge offered to pupils in other areas of mathematics, particularly at KS2, and lead to a failure to recognise that all areas are important and that pupil development is likely to be at different rates in the various ATs – requiring work at different levels in each.

View of mathematics as isolated content blocks

The presentation of mathematics in the document was seen to produce a view of the nature of the subject as made up of completely isolated content blocks. Learning of facts and techniques would receive increased emphasis at the expense of working towards an understanding of the ideas. Although each idea was represented in the PoS or the SoAs, the response to 'too much to get through' and the need to 'tick the boxes' suggested pressures of coverage might well produce an undesirable result. This view was supported by the comment of an interview teacher: 'Nowadays you have to do that number of topics, because you have to tick the number of boxes.'

Such an approach might be seen to promote an instrumental approach to teaching and learning rather than a relational one (Skemp, 1976) – teaching which focuses on performing the algorithms rather than understanding the underlying concepts. The outcome of this was seen to produce short-term learning of items of content rather than building up conceptual relationships.

The teacher groups commented on their own growing awareness of the interweaving of mathematical ideas. This had a positive effect on their planning, giving them the confidence to organise learning experiences which cut across ATs and incorporated elements of UAM. In some cases this was extended to cross-subject curricular activity; for example, map work in geography incorporating related aspects of mathematics. The outcome of these approaches was a way of viewing the mathematics curriculum as manageable and much less of a 'hurdle race', as described by many of the teacher-group participants' colleagues.

Effect of Information Technology

IT was deemed to have a great deal to offer in supporting learning and teaching in mathematics. However the emphasis in the mathematics document was placed upon using the tools, e.g. use a calculator or use a database, rather than aiding pupils in choosing the appropriate tool for doing the mathematics. This was not the case in general, for example, the document did not state 'use a ruler to measure'. In many cases, in both Ma2 (number) and Ma5 (handling data), there were instances in which the SoAs involved the use of prescribed IT tools, and yet the mathematics could be carried out in many ways. The use of a particular IT tool alone for developing understanding of a concept might be deemed necessary, but this was often considered as 'not sufficient'. For example, using only the LOGO environment for drawing a square or considering angle as an amount of turn was felt to construct boundaries of thought about the concept of angle. Both static and dynamic models of the concept of angle were considered important, each having their place in developing conceptual understanding. The PoS and SoAs in general did not offer this model of approach to developing geometrical concepts.

The evidence over the last ten years has demonstrated that as IT tools increase in number and sophistication their appropriate use was likely to shift the emphasis from learning the necessary facts and skills for a particular aspect of mathematics to learning about inter-related mathematical concepts. The use of tools which model the mathematics, such as basic and graphical calculators, geometry software and spreadsheets, indicates that the progression in mathematical content, and its use and applications, might be approached in different ways often leading to a modified hierarchy of knowledge, skills and understandings. It was proposed that this evidence offered potential for a reconsideration of the 'big ideas' which underpin progression in mathematics and the appropriate pedagogy to support their development.

EARLY WORK

In the first month of the project we asked all the teachers in the teacher groups to write about their own and their colleagues' decisions about adapting the NC to their school needs. This writing reflected their initial approaches and attitudes to the givens within the documents. The major concern that came through in their early writing was the need for accommodation and accountability – to accommodate the NC into their own curriculum and to be able to account to others that the full curriculum was being delivered. The writing showed that there was no time for challenge, no space for disagreement, no opportunity for questioning, in fact it seemed that there was no encouragement through the documentation for the teachers to be professionals. For the most part the content of the mathematics NC was taken to be correct, or perhaps not meant to be challenged. One possible account for this was that the curriculum was put into schools with the assessment scheme to follow in a very short time. The teachers were expected to make the contents of the document work, as their pupils were to be tested on it and measured against others. Their writing and discussions indicated how little feeling of 'ownership' existed.

In schools where schemes were used to determine a teaching sequence, the scheme was checked for best fit and alterations made where necessary. As one primary teacher pointed out, 'in published schemes progression is largely dictated'. A secondary teacher remarked: 'the matching of the resources to the attainment targets was done in the main by SMP.' Similar comments came from others in the group, both the primary and the secondary teachers: 'we didn't need to modify our maths policy/programme of study very much after the introduction of the National Curriculum, as it was already a fairly close match . . . we introduced Cambridge [a primary scheme] last year because it seemed to cover the National Curriculum fairly comprehensively.' Another secondary teacher commented:

> In reality the cost factor obviously had a major influence over the final key stage three scheme of work. Since 1987 the school has invested over £5,000 in our new scheme . . . rather than the National Curriculum dictating the school's scheme of work, the resources were matched to fit the National Curriculum.

Having looked for matches and best fit it was the sequence within the NC that was taken to be correct, despite the fact that some in the group had been using their chosen scheme for some years. For example, the comment was made

In my experience I have found that the SMP [secondary] books tend to jump around a lot rather than follow the progression throughout the National Curriculum levels in shape . . . and [in particular] as for rotational symmetry that comes much later on [in the scheme]. This is an area that I am intending to write a scheme of work around to follow the levels of National Curriculum more closely.

Another secondary teacher, talking about checking the statements in the NC against her own teaching syllabus, noted that

this exercise highlighted several areas which are not adequately covered in years 7–9 by our scheme of work . . . I then concentrated on the shape strand in particular . . . I felt that there was certainly an order in which some topic should be covered and I displayed this diagrammatically – the arrows representing progression within the shape strand.

The diagram given was based *exactly* upon the SoAs within the NC. This teacher had rewritten her scheme to fit with the NC. Similarly the primary members of the group accepted the NC and 'fitted' it to the resources in the school, though as the following primary teacher indicated he had to break the givens into more manageable parts:

At my school we now use a syllabus which we drew up 'in house' as a response to the first showing of the maths document. Our syllabus presents a number of themes, and it is intended that any given class will work on a theme for two to three weeks . . . We chose to go for three separate themes as we felt that it made it clearer to the teacher what sort of progression ought to be looked for . . . By giving staff a more refined version, and limiting what they are attempting to cover, we feel we have been able to raise everybody's awareness of where our pupils are going and why.

One of the group reported that her early-years colleagues had ignored most of the NC material and, as a consequence, 'when the Yr2 teachers filled in the teacher assessments prior to the SATs there were gaps in the work covered. However can we blame teachers who had to digest three documents?' Here the idea of 'gaps' assumed the NC was not to be argued with but was there to be implemented almost without question. However, this same teacher also talked about the lack of agreement on progression in terms of 'what goes where': 'this has been a point of debate within the school . . . For example, does 2-D come before 3-D within the Level 1 work in shape and space?'

There was also the expectation that the document would be useful for teachers as a formative assessment guide to help them take decisions on teaching: 'most of the children's work fell within Level 1 but within that level there was a wide continuum of ability, in fact assigning a level to a child tells me very little about what they can actually do and is therefore of little value as a diagnostic tool' (primary teacher). Even as an assessment tool it was limited: 'In fact with very young children I have found that just because they recognise a triangle, for example, in one context doesn't mean that they will recognise it in another or in fact a week later' (primary teacher).

Their early writing showed little criticism of the sequencing within the NC. It was therefore not surprising that during the first year of our meetings the main focus of our discussions was in trying to make sense of the model in terms of the words used and levels attached. External validation was looked for – what do they want? What do they mean? What do they want us to do? As it turned out what was happening was that we were getting to know the model, its possibilities and limitations. Time was needed to make sense of the given curriculum. Initial criticisms were cautious, frustrations arose when the model was thought not to be wholly sensible. The following sections indicate some of the areas of concern that the teachers raised. For the most part they serve the dual role of identifying the weaknesses of the Order whilst at the same time the expectations (sometimes unrealistic) of the teachers.

The differing functions of the PoS and the SoAs

The teachers suggested that in order to form a solid basis of mathematical learning it was often necessary to keep coming back to and extending ideas which had been introduced earlier. Placing similar PoS statements *alongside* SoAs, i.e. placing the planning of the experiences and the measuring of attainment at the same level, did not encourage this. For example:

- PoS, Level 5: 'finding areas of plane figures (excluding circles) using appropriate formulae.'

The teacher groups indicated that these formulae were introduced earlier in their own teaching programme and hence did not appear to be at the right level to correspond to their order of teaching. This PoS statement occurs at the same level as the assessment statement 5d: 'find areas of plane shapes . . .':

- PoS, Level 3: 'sorting 2-D and 3-D shapes and giving reasons for each method of sorting.'

The teacher groups indicated that such activities did, and in their opinion should, begin much earlier. Again this statement is alongside 3a: 'sort shapes using mathematical criteria and give reasons.'

Another example of this was the placing of the assessment of subtraction at Level 2 in the number target. Subtraction was also first mentioned in Level 2 of the PoS for number. The primary teachers agreed that first ideas about subtraction should be explored at Level 1 with assessment coming later. A final example could be seen in Level 7 of Ma4 (see Table 4.2). Like the teaching of subtraction the teachers expressed concern that in order to assess a pupil's ability to determine the locus of an object, activities relating to this should be started at a much earlier level.

Evidence from APU (1985) and the research programme CSMS (Hart, 1981) would suggest that learning takes place over a period of time and in a range of

Table 4.2 A comparison of PoS and SoAs within Ma4 Level 7 (complete)

PoS: 'pupils should engage in activities which involve . . .'	SoAs: 'pupils should be able to do . . .'
• using co-ordinates to locate position in 3-D	a) Use co-ordinates (x, y, z) to locate position in 3-D
• determining the locus of an object moving subject to a rule	b) Determine the locus of an object which is moving subject to a rule
• understanding and applying Pythagoras' theorem	c) Use Pythagoras' theorem
• using knowledge and skills in length, area and volume to carry out calculations in plane and solid shapes	d) Carry out calculations in plane and solid shapes
• enlarging a shape by a fractional scale factor	

contexts before reaching 'mastery' understanding. Placing the learning alongside the assessment did not encourage this view of learning, especially if the teaching and assessment objective were seen to be identical. The teachers felt that the presentation did not encourage a spiral curriculum and indeed since the Order was a legal requirement this might actually encourage the view that the teaching of a concept only begins at the level first mentioned in the PoS. The document therefore also assumed an expertness that non-expert teachers might follow and could actually encourage a teaching style mainly of exposition plus practice followed by an assessment task. This could lead to apparent student progress, but as research evidence has indicated the skills acquired in this way are not reliably retained by most pupils nor are they transferable to non-routine problems (Bassford, 1989).

The relationship between the PoS and the SoAs not clearly defined

In the 1991 revision of the 1989 Order some statements were kept in the assessment structure, some removed and some new ones written to cover a 'clutch' of PoS statements. Analysis of the targets seemed to show an arbitrary collection of statements, which would become problematic if the external assessment (of the SoAs) was used to determine pupil attainment. One of the issues raised was illustrated with Ma4 Level 7 (Table 4.2). Each of the PoS statements was replicated in the assessment structure *except* for the final PoS statement on enlarging by a scale factor. Reasons for the exclusion were not clear. The non-reference of this statement could be taken as a reflection of its mathematical importance in relation to the other statements. This had consequences for those constructing a teaching programme. *Choices* might be made from the PoS for a teaching programme with outcomes based on SoAs.

The teachers were concerned that assessment statements that were an exact repetition of PoS statements (some were not) would be seen as more important in the curriculum because of their placing in the assessment structure and therefore affect the understanding of the PoS as a coherent planning model. The teachers also expressed the view that certain topics were under-represented in the chosen assessment statements, e.g. angle and transformation geometry.

Attributes within a statement not of equal difficulty

When we came to look at whether or not the statements were consistent with one another we discovered that they were not. Maybe we had to make this initial discovery before asking the next question about whether it was possible to define statements that were consistent and of equal difficulty. The initial comments from the teachers raised issues about comparability – the teachers assumed that the attributes within statements should be of the same order of difficulty. For example:

- PoS, Level 1: 'building with 3-D solid shapes and drawing 2-D shapes and describing them.'

This statement had four attributes. The teachers thought that describing 3-D shapes was more difficult than building 3-D shapes or drawing 2-D shapes or even describing 2-D shapes. A similar problem of comparability was identified in an evaluation project of NC assessment at KS1 (SEAC, 1992), which tested this particular statement about 2-D and 3-D shapes. The results from the report indicated that the attribute 'describe 3-D shapes' was significantly more difficult than the other three. Ninety-two per cent of the children attained the SoA when the three-attribute interpretation was used, whereas only 79 per cent attained this when all four attributes were required.

There were many other examples in the document, e.g.:

- PoS, Level 3: 'recognising (reflective) symmetry in a variety of shapes in two and three dimensions.'

The attribute 'recognising reflective symmetry in 3-D' was thought to be much more difficult than recognising it in 2-D. The SoA alongside the above PoS statement was 'recognise reflective symmetry'.

Many of the teachers indicated that they were interpreting these statements through the PoS statements, i.e. 3a: 'recognise reflective symmetry' was equated with the PoS Level 3 statement 'recognise reflective symmetry . . . in two and three dimensions'. If such assumptions were being made then assessing the SoA could also become problematic, particularly if all the attributes were to be attained. Notice that concerns were about the fairness of assessment. Thoughts about invalid paper-and-pencil tests were beginning to dominate discussions.

Comparability of statements within a level

In any level of any of the ATs some of the statements were conceptually more difficult than others. For example in Level 7 of Ma4 (see Table 4.2), 'using 3-D co-ordinates . . .' was felt by the teacher group to be a significantly different type of statement from 'determining the locus . . .'. Finding a locus demands many skills and concepts. Using 3-D co-ordinates is a useful representational skill. At the moment the SAT assessment gave equal weighting to each statement although vastly different time periods were required to 'master' these two statements.

The teachers raised many questions about the comparable difficulty of statements within a level. Does a level contain statements of varied difficulty or the same difficulty? Should there be progression within a level? This problem was highlighted in some SEAC evaluation data. The results (Table 4.3) from the KS3 SATs pilot (CATS, 1991) showed the range of attainment across a level from the teacher assessments given. Table 4.3 indicates the percentages for each statement within a level and provides a graph of this distribution. The marked difference in attainment of statements across a level occurred most noticeably at Levels 5, 6 and 7 where the range of pupils attaining the statements must call into question the notional equivalence of the statements. At Level 5, for example, 45.7 per cent of pupils were able to attain 'identify symmetry of various shapes' whilst only 17.2 per cent were able to 'specify location in the four quadrants'. At Level 6, 42.8 per cent could 'reflect simple shapes in a mirror line' whilst only 8.8 per cent could 'devise instructions for a computer to produce desired shapes'. Although such statements were now part of the PoS, nevertheless this offered an indication as to the possible ranges that might exist between the same level statements (whilst acknowledging that reasons for this range were not clear from the data).

Table 4.3 Teacher assessments: percentages of pupils attaining each SoA in AT11*

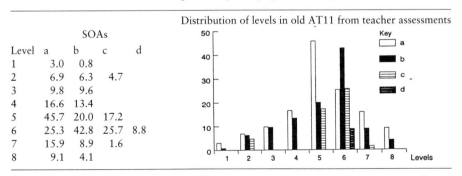

Distribution of levels in old AT11 from teacher assessments

	SOAs			
Level	a	b	c	d
1	3.0	0.8		
2	6.9	6.3	4.7	
3	9.8	9.6		
4	16.6	13.4		
5	45.7	20.0	17.2	
6	25.3	42.8	25.7	8.8
7	15.9	8.9	1.6	
8	9.1	4.1		

Note: * 1989 Order. Percentages of pupils attaining each SoA at the earlier levels were low as teachers were instructed not to record SoAs below the level at which all SoAs had been attained for each pupil. Valid comparisons could not therefore be made between percentages of pupils attaining SoAs at different levels.

Effect of resources on the apparent difficulty of a statement

There was concern from the teacher groups about the use of computers affecting the difficulty of the mathematics within a statement. For example:

- PoS, Level 6: 'using computers to generate and transform 2-D shapes' and its equivalent SoA 6b: 'Transform shapes using a computer, or otherwise.'

The 1991 KS3 SAT pilot showed that 7.5 per cent of KS3 pupils attained this statement compared with 19.9, 24.3 and 18.6 per cent for the other space and shapes statements at this level. This may have been a consequence of lack of resources or teachers' lack of confidence and experience in handling them rather than the mathematics assessed being particularly difficult.

Effect of context on the apparent difficulty of a statement

The effect of context on attainment was also discussed by the teacher groups. Interpretations of a statement to be tested within different contexts could result in different levels being attained. How many examples would be sufficient to place a statement in a level? In how many contexts should a pupil be seen to be achieving the statement before he or she was said to be able to do that aspect of mathematics?

The 1991 KS3 SATs pilot tested various attainment targets in two contexts, 'Gift packs' and 'Octagon loops'. AT10 (space and shape, 1989 Order) was assessed in both tasks. The figures given for the distribution of attainment (see Table 4.4) indicated the type of variation that might be expected as the context of the assessment varied. There was quite a wide range attaining the statements within a level in the two different tasks. For example the percentage of pupils attaining Level 6 in the 'Octagon loop' task was higher than that in the 'Gift pack' task. It was impossible to say which task if any reflected more accurately the attainment of the pupils.

Table 4.4 Comparison of AT10 (SoAs) using 'Gift packs' and 'Octagon loops'*

AT10 (SoAs) – Gift packs					AT10 (SoAs) – Octagon loops				
Level	a	b	c	d	Level	a	b	c	d
1	3.7	2.8			1	1.2	2.5		
2	6.4	8.6			2	7.3	6.0		
3	13.7				3	17.1			
4	25.6	31.4			4	11.9	26.6		
5	19.5	23.7			5	20.5	37.1		
6	16.6	24.7	0.4	10.9	6	20.8	1.0	7.2	16.8
7	6.3				7	8.4			
8	3.3				8	5.3			
9	0.8	0.5	0.2		9	0.2	0.9	0.4	
10	0.0	0.0	0.0	0.0	10	0.0	0.1	0.0	0.0

Note: * See footnote for Table 4.3.

Specificity of statements

Learning that the document would not hold all the answers to decisions about a teaching programme took a while. We discovered that many of the statements in the document were ambiguous and the examples insufficient to determine what was meant or intended to be taught/learnt as a consequence. Consider, for example:

- Level 4, SoA: 'Construct 2-D and 3-D shapes and know associated language.'

Depending on apparatus used, task set and guidance given, a variety of tasks at differing levels of demand might be created. Also there was no obvious progression in terms of learning outcomes between this statement and the SoA at the next level, 'Use accurate measurement and drawing in constructing 3-D models'. The examples given at both levels contained the suggestion to 'construct prisms' without any indication of the progression expected.

The teachers also found that certain statements lacked clarity. For example:

- Level 1, SoA: 'Compare and order objects without measuring.'

Measuring needed more careful definition since comparison and ordering were seen by the teachers as aspects of measurement and therefore required some understanding of measurement in order to be carried out. Being told that these things happen without measurement needed careful thought.

- PoS, Level 2: 'recognising right-angled corners in 2-D and 3-D shapes.'

The phrase 'right angle' was used at this level whereas 'square corner' was used in the 'example' given for Level 3. It seemed inappropriate to introduce the dynamic terminology of 'right angle' so early in the development of the concept of angular measure.

Many of the statements in the Order were not specific and not limited to aspects of a general mathematical aim but part of the general aims. Consider the following three statements:

- SoA, Level 4, number: 'Solve problems without the aid of a calculator, . . .'
- SoA, Level 6, algebra: 'Solve simple (linear) equations.'
- SoA, Level 4, handling data: 'Interrogate and interpret data in a computer database.'

Each of these statements could be placed at almost any level in the Order. For this reason placing many of the statements at a level required much work and interpretation by the teacher. As already mentioned in the section above such statements are 'huge', requiring the teacher to make many decisions in order to unpack the level of cognitive demand. What information was used to place each of these statements at a particular level? What behaviours should a pupil exhibit? What teaching should be constructed? Some actions that the teacher groups took to try to give a statement meaning were

- consider the PoS statements,
- consider the SoAs in the adjacent levels, and
- consider the examples which accompanied the SoAs.

(There was a fourth option, an extension of using the examples, and that was to use the SAT questions where available.) The linking of these three actions is illustrated in Table 4.5, the SoAs for Ma5/4a as related to 3a and 5a, i.e. the levels just before and just after 4a.

Table 4.5   Statements* for Ma5/4a related to 3a and 5a

SoAs →	Related PoS →	Examples
3a: Access information in a simple database	Entering and accessing information in a simple database, e.g. card database	(*not directly related*) Handle weather statistics or personal data, . . .
↑		
4a: Interrogate and interpret data in a computer database →	Inserting, interrogating and interpreting data in a computer database	Interrogate a simple database to find plants suitable for creating a garden border which flowers blue and white in the summer months
↓		
5a: Use a computer database to draw conclusions	Inserting and interrogating data in a computer database; drawing conclusions	Draw conclusions from census data about the effect of an epidemic/ industrial revolution/ changes in transport

Note: * There were no SAT questions relating to this statement. This was one of the many statements that could not be assessed by a timed written test.

Three main points seemed to emerge from our analysis of the components in Table 4.5: 1) the PoS statements seemed to repeat the SoAs and offered no further help except for the reference to a card base in Level 3; 2) this particular example appeared to have an element of progression within the AT, however, this did not appear to be the case for many of the statements. The statements at Levels 3 and 5 did not help much to exemplify the Level 4 statement. The Level 3 SoA used 'simple' database and by reference to the PoS statement this was perhaps a card database. Level 4 was explicitly referred to as a computer database. Level 5 however did not advance a notion of progression. Its reference to 'draw conclusions' was the difference at this level but the teachers decided that drawing conclusions was something required by the example in Level 4 about flowers; and 3) the examples were confusing since the example at Level 4 referred to a simple database which were the words used to describe the database at Level 3. The intended problem described at Level 5 might have been perceived to be more difficult though this was dependent on the problem posed and the question asked and these were not included.

The use of poor examples could actually trivialise the mathematics curriculum if more was attributed to the example than was intended by the writers. Poor SAT questions could hold similar power.

As in this case of databases the document alone did not offer sufficient definition for the statement to attain meaning. Consistency and 'right level' could not be attributed to the document other than superficially. The teacher group attempted to rewrite some of these statements with greater clarity. This proved not to be feasible as either the curriculum became too restricted by the limitations placed upon the statement in order to agree meaning or else the statement required a great deal of written explanation creating a cumbersome document. However, the group decided that the curriculum needed such statements, and further

- such statements would need a wider use of examples than currently existed (but not as part of the Order) to give meaning and interpretation, and
- the general aims (such as solve problems without a calculator or solve linear equations) should have been part of a PoS – particular SoAs would need to be written to represent a specific aspect of a target at a particular level.

Reflecting back it is interesting how the project questions determined a way of working. We were asked to consider 'whether SoAs were at the right level and consistent with one another' rather than was it possible or even sensible to select and define a sequence. Presumably such questions had been answered by the groups of professionals who had been part of the working groups who had put the original Order and the revised Order together (stemming from the report by TGAT (DES/WO, 1987)). As I look back on our early work it is not surprising that we were trying to find the 'right' sequence of statements, the 'right' wording for each of the statements, the 'right' placing of statements, and statements that offered a more thorough explanation of intention.

A POINT IN TIME: MOVING INTO THE SECOND YEAR

As we moved into the second year it became clear that looking for a 'rightness' was a fruitless journey. We had come to understand the possibilities and limitations of the model we were analysing. Sufficient confidence had grown for the teachers to develop their own examples to accompany the statements, to make the statements make sense and have meaning at a particular level. The teachers felt that they had sufficient understanding of the model to give it meaning without exclusive reference to outside agencies. The perception of the mathematics presented in the Order also changed as the groups attempted to look for the relationship of mathematical ideas across the targets and within the targets whilst looking to use the Order to help create a mathematics curriculum for their pupils. The groups were also concerned with trying to understand the differences between general teaching aims that they felt should be present in the PoS and specific assessment criteria which underpinned the SoAs in the assessment structure, and ways that these might both be presented in the Order.

At the start of the second year our discussion focused on the handling-data strand. It is worth offering some of the results from these discussions as they represent the move from the correctness of the document into different ways of thinking about progression in this AT. Some of the issues raised were similar to those raised previously but I think that we realised such issues were bound to be present. More generally, reactions from the groups were that

- developmental links were missing or not evident;
- the handling-data target appeared to be a collection of techniques placed at arbitrary levels; and
- progression was not evident within the AT except as an attempt to make sure that everything was covered.

Looking through the statements, the first point identified by the teachers was that many things appeared in later levels which should be in the earlier ones or indeed that should be in every one. For example, consider the following SoAs:

- Level 4: 'Conduct a survey on an issue of their choice.'
- Level 5: 'Design and use an observation sheet to collect data.'
- Level 6: 'Design and use a questionnaire to survey opinion.'
- Level 7: 'Organise and analyse data.'
- Level 8: 'Design and use a questionnaire or experiment to test a hypothesis.'

Placing any one of these statements at a particular level (as was done) gave the impression, rightly or wrongly, that they were therefore excluded from the other levels. Also, the teachers in the group reported that the activities described in the examples at the higher levels were also carried out by pupils as early as KS1. As a result the examples did not offer sufficient explanation of progression through the levels, e.g. consider the examples given at Levels 4 and 5:

- Level 4: 'Find and record the number of pupils born in each month . . .'; 'Conduct a survey across the school to find which five events . . .'
- Level 5: 'Conduct a survey of cars passing with one, two, three . . . occupants.'

The primary teachers recognised these as activities carried out at earlier levels though actual pupil outcomes would differ depending on the age and attainment level.

The teachers felt that each of these statements and examples might be happening *throughout* learning about handling data and unlike in the work in the previous year they began to take the initiative with the curriculum to work on this.

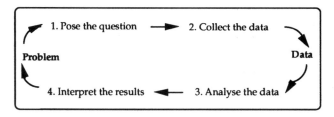

Figure 4.1 The handling-data cycle

First, they did some work with their pupils to justify their reactions. For example a Yr3 class conducted a survey as part of a trip to the Science Museum. Problems occurred when pupils were asked to consider posing and phrasing a question to be answered. For example the pupils did not immediately see what they would not be able to measure, e.g. speed of car, and tried to work with too many variables, e.g. number of passengers and colour of car and sunroof. However the pupils were able to engage with the idea of posing questions (the beginning of setting hypotheses). They conducted their own survey, designed their own observation sheets in the process and used their results to answer the questions they had posed. Some of these pupils predicted their answers and set up an experiment to test their ideas.

A Yr1 class had to choose the name for the class goldfish. They conducted a survey to choose some names, selected three names and then voted for their favourite name. This Yr1 class was involved in many of the statements previously described. A Yr7 and 9 class were also engaged in the full handling-data cycle (see Figure 4.1).

Having satisfied themselves that their initial reactions were accurate and appropriate, the task for the teachers then became one of identifying the significant difference in moving from one level to another level and finding reasons or explanations for the placement of certain statements at particular levels. To begin thinking about this further, at the second meeting the groups looked for alternative models to describe this AT. They felt that the handling-data statements were neither at the 'right' nor the 'wrong' levels and so an attempt was made not to reorganise, but to rethink. Could we have reached this stage without the early analysis of the model? This was a different way of working from our earlier analyses. Did we have greater confidence of the task in hand or perhaps a growing belief that shifting statements would not necessarily produce a more correct model of the curriculum? A possible flow for handling data was discussed by the groups. This was close to the model described in *Handling Data* (OU, 1991), given in Figure 4.1.

Posing and answering questions were fundamental to this flow and yet were absent for the most part within the curriculum Order. Posing a question or trying to answer a given question would help determine, and give a reason for determining, a sensible choice for sample size, data-collection format and style of representation: 'as a result of working through the full cycle the pupils might come to see data handling techniques (graphs, the calculation of averages and so on) as genuinely useful skills that can help them to answer questions which *they* might pose for themselves' (OU, 1991, p. 6).

The examples given against the SoAs had no questions as a starting point. For example:

- Level 2: 'Collect data on children who walk to school and those who travel by bus, . . .'
- Level 3: 'Handle weather statistics; find the cost of an item in a mail order catalogue, . . .'
- Level 4: 'Find and record the number of pupils born in each month of the year, . . .'
- Level 5: 'Conduct a survey of cars passing with one, two, three . . . occupants.'

Many of the words used to describe the different points in this handling-data cycle were also to be found in the first AT of the mathematics curriculum, UAM. For example, the pupils are required to make decisions about the problem, the data, how best to represent and communicate, how to generalise from an initial hypothesis. (This cycle is not particular to mathematics nor indeed are the statistical skills defined in this AT. Science, for example, refers to many of the statements in the mathematics PoS.)

Many questions arose as a consequence of our discussions. Could the PoS be written in such a way that such a cycle would provide the framework for learning useful techniques? Could the examples be placed in this framework? What about posing questions from across the curriculum? What would it mean to pose a harder question? What about increasing the number of variables or changing the types of data from discrete to continuous? What concepts should be developed as the pupil gets better at collecting, analysing and interpreting data? What might lead to an understanding of ideas of sampling, bias, validity, etc.? Table 4.6 presents the ideas that the teachers put together as an initial flow for working on handling data.

The group were keen that this cycle was evident in the PoS and reflected in the SoAs. At Level 1, for example, the pupils should be posing their own questions as well as responding to questions given, collecting data, making predictions and using the data to come to decisions. The role of teaching would then become one of enabling the pupils to answer their own questions. The group pondered on how the role of the teacher might be exemplified in the PoS. Collecting data at this level would be by show of hands, simple sorting, groupings and observation sheets. Analysis would then come in using the data to answer the question. Naming the goldfish in the Yr1 class became an exemplification of this approach.

At Level 2 pupils should be encouraged to pose their own questions, design a data-collecting sheet and method of recording. The pupils should be encouraged to see the need to collect and record results, to organise their data to find

Table 4.6 A possible progression for the handling-data strand (Ma5) – collecting and analyzing

1. Posing the question 2. Collecting the data:	3. Analysing the data *Processing the data*
• collecting through observation –physically collecting –relating to classrooms –distinguishing features/differences • one-to-one recording from observation, e.g. tally charts and tables • collecting by asking questions • thinking about the sample – limitations, bias, comparing samples • collecting continuous data • data from questionnaires – options, bias, trends	• counting • representative value(s) • considering mean as a representative value • range • grouping, considering distribution • cumulative frequency • line of best fit, inter-quartile range, percentile, standard deviation *Representing the data:* • actual groupings – show of hands, circles, sets • physical representation, i.e. symbolising the groupings — block graphs, cube per person • one-to-one pictorial representation – pictograms, block charts • abstract representation, idea of scale – bar chart, line graph, pie chart, scatter graph
4. Interpreting the data	

the 'best' way to record and communicate findings. The Yr3 class's visit to the Science Museum and traffic survey followed this cycle with the pupils setting their own questions within certain constraints set by the teacher.

Table 4.6 represented a first attempt at thinking about progression within an aspect of mathematics. Unlike the earlier work we moved away from finding fault with the model and tried to think about alternatives. Many ideas were debated. It was interesting that the suggestions put forward contained statements that were just as ambiguous, if not more so, than many of the statements we had analysed in the previous year, but these had taken on a shared meaning or interpretation for the teachers in the groups.

DISCUSSION

It seems that offering teachers a curriculum and asking them to make sense of it over time is nothing unusual. In fact the opposite is true. The blank curriculum is a concept that few of us have had opportunity to work with. In primary and secondary schools, schemes abound, and at the secondary level 16-plus examination syllabuses have determined teaching programmes for a long time. What became evident in this project and crucial to the teachers was the need for time to make sense of an external curriculum and time to integrate it into a particular school's needs and resources.

The teachers in the group worked in three phases over time:

1. Trying to accommodate the (assumed) givens without questioning.
2. Making sense of the (assumed) givens.
3. Trying to accommodate the (now personally interpreted) givens within their own frameworks for teaching and learning.

As can be seen from the discussion about the work during the second year, by the end of the time spent considering progression in the handling-data AT we were more prepared to begin considering progression in the associated mathematics. The teachers were confident about their own abilities to determine what statements might mean at a level, more confident to be less literal about the wording of the Order, confident to enjoy ambiguity if within the group there was support to be found for what was happening in their classrooms, and confident in their ability and professional right, or even obligation, to question, argue and debate.

As for progression, the possibility of defining progression in an abstract form unrelated to age remains a huge challenge. As the working group had reported, back in 1988, '[they] were breaking new ground in attempting to develop a mathematics curriculum with continuity and progression through from the primary reception class to the secondary fifth' (DES/WO, 1988, p. 1). The teacher groups could now agree on macro-progressions, e.g. linear equations before differential equations, addition and subtraction before the Pythagorean theorem. Micro-progressions are the day-to-day decisions that arise from working with real pupils in real classrooms with the particular resources available. Working on the topic of 'area' is important but who minds whether I work with the area of a parallelogram before the area of a triangle or vice versa? The model of the NC initially set us a 'rightness' that, when considered in terms of our initial expectations, we agreed failed, even if the rightness was not intentional. Moving from NC level to level, and having moved from one level to leave that content behind is not consistent with the experience of classroom teachers. For the teachers, learning is cyclic not linear and takes place over time – beginning to know – knowing – knowing more. We arrived at the end of the project with our professionalism reasserted and the feeling of a high degree of 'ownership' of the curriculum – maybe now is the time for us to begin to consider the nature of progression in school mathematics.

5

'USING AND APPLYING MATHEMATICS' IN SCHOOLS: READING THE TEXTS

Mike Askew
King's College London

The focus of this chapter is on differing 'readings' of NC texts produced as part of the mandatory introduction of a problem-solving and investigative strand – 'Using and Applying Mathematics' – into the English and Welsh mathematics curriculum. Analysis of interview data gives insight into teachers' readings of this aspect of the curriculum. These readings are contrasted with the curriculum implications as might be read into the policy documents from those within the mathematics education community.

INTRODUCTION

The argument developed here is broadly in line with that adopted by Bowe, Ball and Gold (1992) in that simple uni-directional relationships between policy generation and implementation in terms of top-down or bottom-up models of curriculum development are rejected. Instead, policy is regarded as discourse with various texts capable of being read with a variety of interpretations. From this position of policy as discourse, there is no essentially 'true' reading of the texts against which various positions can be judged, thus rejecting the view that teachers have a deficit model of the NC requirements. This chapter explores the interplay of policy and practice, taking 'Using and Applying Mathematics' as a key case. (Throughout the capitalised Using and Applying Mathematics or UAM will be used to signify the NC sense of these words as explicated below.)

Arguments and initiatives aimed at the need for changes to the mathematics curriculum are not new. Changes away from a narrow focus on basic techniques, in particular operations upon number, towards more attention on mathematical thinking processes and problem-solving are frequently advocated (Cockcroft, 1982). But progress in this direction has generally been slow and uneven. For example, in England, PrIME, the Primary Initiatives in Mathematics Education Project (1985–89) (Shuard *et al.*, 1990), an extensive cascade model of curriculum development, had patchy success. Similarly the introduction of mathematical investigations through GCSE coursework has had varied impact on the rest of the curriculum (Jaworski, 1994).

Now the introduction of a mathematics NC for England and Wales has potentially altered the situation. An assessment schedule of five ATs each equally weighted, with the inclusion of mathematics AT1 (Ma1) UAM and an associated teaching PoS, requires teachers to make provision for pupils to engage in nonroutine mathematical activities located both within mathematics itself and in 'real-life' contexts.[1] The NC has made problem-solving and investigations mandatory.

While investigative and problem-solving aspects of mathematics have at least been firmly marked on the English and Welsh curriculum map, the extent to which these process aspects are manifesting themselves in the landscapes of classrooms is still open to question. Evidence so far suggests that the implementation of these aspects of the curriculum is limited and teaching practices in mathematics little changed as a result of the legislation.

The development of Ma1: 'Using and Applying Mathematics'

In the August 1988 proposals for the mathematics curriculum (DES/WO, 1988) three PCs were suggested, each from a cluster of ATs. The first PC was formed from ATs in number, algebra and measures, the second around shape and space and data handling. The third PC, 'Practical Applications of Mathematics', laid the foundations of what would ultimately become Ma1. Within this PC, three ATs were proposed: using mathematics, communication skills and personal qualities. The proposals contained comments on PC3 being essentially 'practical in nature' but already there was a sense that the proposed title 'Practical Applications of Mathematics' did not fully capture the flavour of the content of the ATs which went beyond everyday, real-life applications of mathematics to also consider the abstract and symbolic.

The December Consultation Report (NCC, 1988, p. 7), arising out of the August proposals, indicated that a first task had been to 're-examine and, where possible, combine the attainment targets and associated statements of attainment for the practical applications of mathematics, with the targets for knowledge and understanding'. As there were still to be two PCs concerned with content, the proposed solution to this combining was to have two ATs, 1 and 9, each with identical SoAs but with foci on different mathematical contexts. Each would be called 'Using and Applying Mathematics' but AT1 would be about 'using number, algebra and measures in practical tasks and real-life problems' while AT9 would involve 'using shape and space and handling data in practical tasks and real-life problems'. These two ATs still had explicit emphases on using mathematics and communication skills, many SoAs from the proposed PC3 still being included. However, the proposed PC3 'Personal Qualities' attainment target was less easily identifiable as a strand within the new ATs1 and 9.

ATs1 and 9 as presented in the 1989 Order (DES/WO, 1989a) were largely unaltered from those suggested in the December Consultation Report. The most notable change was to the 'subhead' by the inclusion of explicit reference to investigating mathematics – AT1: 'Pupils should use number, algebra and measures in practical tasks, in real-life problems, and to investigate within mathematics itself' (*ibid.*, p. 3) – similarly for AT9 within the contexts of shape and space and data handling. The NSG accompanying the Order reiterated that ATs1 and 9 'Using and Applying Mathematics' were about using mathematics and communicating in mathematics but also addressed a third aspect: 'developing ideas of argument and proof' (DES/WO, 1989b, p. D2). These explicit references to the purely mathematical and the implications of working with the abstract meant that the title 'Using and Applying Mathematics' became even less appropriate as a means of conveying the spirit of the ATs. The NSG also emphasised the two-way relationship between ATs1 and 9 and the other ATs, the former being expected to motivate and require the latter. Similarly the 'content' ATs were expected to facilitate and enable the using and applying of mathematics. The model proposed was one of permeation: ATs1 and 9 and their PoS should 'permeate all other work in mathematics, providing both the means to, and the rationale for, the progressive development of knowledge, skills and understanding in mathematics' (*ibid.*, p. D3).

With the Order in place both the NCC and HMI identified that teachers were having difficulty in interpreting the SoAs of ATs1 and 9, particularly in terms of identifying progression (see, for example, HMI, 1991a; NCC, 1991). The 1991 Order and additional NSG attempted to remedy this by making more explicit three strands within the new Ma1: 'Applications, Mathematical communication and Reasoning, logic and proof' (DES/WO, 1991). Ma1 was still, however, to be called 'Using and Applying Mathematics' but an element of the personal qualities re-entered the 'subhead':

> Pupils should choose and make use of knowledge, skills and understanding outlined in the programmes of study in practical tasks, in real-life problems and to investigate within mathematics itself. Pupils would be expected to use with confidence the appropriate mathematical content specified in the programmes of study relating to the other attainment targets.
>
> (*Ibid.*, p. 1)

In the analysis below, teachers' responses are examined in the light of the documents supporting ATs1 and 9 as it was these ATs which, at the time of interview, most teachers were working with. In the 1991 Order, although the SoAs for Ma1 were revised, the PoS statements were largely unaltered from those that accompanied ATs1 and 9. Hence it was reasonable to assume that perceptions and implementation of Ma1 were little changed from the ways in which teachers made sense of ATs1 and 9.

THE STUDY

As indicated in Chapter 2, the aim of the Mathematics Evaluation Project (Askew *et al.*, 1993) was to pursue four areas of concern through a connected set of investigations. One specified area was the implementation of UAM which some commentators saw as presenting a major challenge to the existing mathematics teaching in many schools (HMI, 1991a). Preliminary monitoring of the implementation of the NC for mathematics subjects (NCC, 1991) identified that many teachers were finding the processes of UAM difficult to integrate into their work. The King's evaluation was to examine the reasons why this was so and to identify factors leading to good and successful practice. Findings on the former of these two foci – difficulty of implementation of UAM – are reported here.

The questionnaire

Reasons for difficulty in implementing UAM were initially explored through responses to a questionnaire (see Appendix 1). From analysis of full data sets of 744 responses perceived difficulties in relation to UAM included

- lack of teaching experience of UAM,
- inadequate coverage by commercial schemes,
- lack of clarity in the meaning of UAM in both the AT and PoS, and
- difficulties related to the need for changes in teaching style.

However, although a substantial proportion of teachers surveyed indicated perceived difficulties in the implementation of UAM, the majority of respondents did not regard coverage of this aspect of the mathematics NC as especially problematic. This raised the question of why there should be a discrepancy between teachers' own reporting of the extent of implementation of UAM and other reports of limited evidence of take-up. Interview data provided some insights to help account for this apparent discrepancy

The interviews

Follow-up interviews (see Chapter 2) were based around semi-structured schedules: a number of broad themes were introduced for discussion with the teachers, making clear that the intention was to evaluate the impact of the introduction of the NC rather than judge individuals' teaching styles. Spradley's (1979) categories of 'descriptive', 'structural' and 'contrast' informed the development of the questions and pilot interviews were conducted to frame the questions.

To explore UAM the interviewees were initially asked an open descriptive question: 'Can you give a specific example of a maths activity that you have recently taught which you think involved the children in some aspect of "Using and Applying Mathematics"?' (It was made clear to the teachers that questions in this part of the interview were dealing with the NC interpretation of using and applying.) Depending on whether their response to this question seemed to indicate a practical task, 'real-life' problem or mathematical investigation, a more focused follow-up contrast question was asked, inviting the teacher to describe an activity of a different nature (for example, if a mathematical example was offered, the teacher was asked about practical or 'real-life' examples). Structural questions were based around changes to their practice in this aspect of mathematics since the introduction of the NC and difficulties encountered in providing opportunities for UAM. Each interview lasted at least 45 minutes and many extended to an hour and a half. All the teachers agreed for the interviews to be audio taped.

Interview analysis

The interviews were transcribed and initially open coded and summarised using techniques described by Miles and Huberman (1984) and Strauss (1987). As well as responses to the questions specifically focused on UAM, the transcripts were examined for other instances of references to classroom experiences which might be considered relevant. Coding categories were developed using the constant comparative method (Glaser and Strauss, 1967). On the basis of the codes derived, three networks (Bliss, Monk and Ogborn, 1983) were developed to encapsulate the interconnections of codes and recurrent themes. One network was for teachers of 5–7-year-olds (KS1: R, Yr1 and 2), one for teachers of 7–11-year-olds (KS2: Yr3 to 6) and one for teachers of 11–14-year-olds (KS3: Yr7 to 9).

THE TEXTS OF UAM: TEACHERS' INTERPRETATIONS

Teachers interviewed displayed wide variation in their interpretation of UAM. In turn this appeared to have affected their style and extent of implementation. Many of the teachers appeared to believe that by providing mathematics lessons in which reference was made to the 'real world', pupils must be engaged in UAM. KS1 teachers, particularly but not exclusively, frequently referred to the ubiquity of Ma1, as this reception teacher exemplifies:

Everything around us, yes, and the fact, we take turns to be leaders, who is first in line, who's second, if you don't behave you go to the end of the line, so you're last. Eight pencils counted, well I mean that's obviously what we're doing, the set of eight pencils is counted . . . We've got underlay sheets where you've got eight Unifix arranged in different shapes, so they match them up and then they count each set.

Practical and relevant were two terms which the teachers seemed especially to associate with UAM. While these might appear synonymous with the NC exhortations for the inclusion of 'practical tasks' and 'real-life problems', it emerged that teachers placed particular interpretations on these terms – interpretations that warranted further examination for their implications.

UAM as 'relevant' mathematics

Relevance, in the everyday use of the term, involves some sense of utility. Money is a 'relevant' topic in the mathematics curriculum because of its immediate applicability. For several teachers relevance appeared to come about through a focus on everyday applications: money, measurement in its various forms and day-to-day numeracy form the bulk of examples in the interviews which these teachers gave as UAM. Such relevance seemed a way of appreciating the usefulness of mathematics.

A Yr5 teacher:

Q: Can you give me an example of something they've done [involving using and applying]?
A: Oh, things like shopping lists or adding and dividing and making averages, rounding up and approximating things like that, I think if you can't relate it to life they don't get the meaning of it.

[*Later*] I think its just that I try and make it relevant, and try and make it so that they can see what's happening to them, maybe away from school at home.

But at least two other meanings of relevant were apparent, each less concerned with equipping pupils with necessary life skills. The first involved the drawing-on of experiences outside school as a means of 'disguising' the mathematics being used, a means to 'sugar the pill'.

A Yr2 teacher:

They're using number work in the shop, when they're adding up the prices. I mean I gave them little shopping bills that they had to give to another person, so they're actually doing number work there. Simple addition and subtraction not realising that they are doing it, six take away six or whatever, but they are actually using their number work.

There was also a strong sense that within the context of teaching mathematics, 'relevance' seemed to be related to providing some sort of imagery, practical or verbal, or as a means of motivation. For some teachers this seemed to come about simply by the use of physical materials in lessons with an underlying assumption that as long as real objects (either physically present or imagined) could be invoked then children would find the activity relevant, no matter how 'unreal' the mathematics they were required to do with the objects.

A Yr5 teacher:

> I think it's just that I try and make it relevant, and try and make it so that they can see what's happening to them, maybe away from school, at home. I'm heavily into Smarties and toffees. Anything that they can sort of visualise and think 'oh yes, I fancy that so. . . .'

This teacher, like others, saw the tasks as needing purpose from the teacher's point of view, but not necessarily the pupils'. In response to a question about whether the pupils ever chose the mathematics or apparatus, she replied:

> I don't think so, because of the limit of language, it's got to be a task which is set, that you can see a purpose in. Maybe they don't see the purpose themselves, or see why you're using particular apparatus, so I wouldn't actually say that they have a choice.

There was little indication from interviews that the teachers thought pupils could find relevance in activities that may not have some immediate practical application, again appearing to reflect an emphasis on the title of the AT rather than the detail. Thus there is a potential conflict between the interpretation of using and applying as 'relevant' in this sense of everyday applicability and relevant in the sense of intellectually engaging.

While the mathematics NC texts may specify a focus on mathematical process skills, there was little evidence of this reading in the teachers' accounts. Only one teacher (of Yr6) talked about the processes of reasoning logic and proof and was the only teacher to offer an example chosen with this specifically in mind:

> Yes, the prime numbers for example . . . Some of it wasn't really using Ma1, in that they were given a specific way of doing it, and they had, you know, take multiples of two and colour them in and that sort of thing, so that they were actually directed into what they were doing. But once they'd done that they were given a statement and they had to try and prove whether it was correct or not and they had to draw conclusions from the result.

UAM as 'practical' mathematics

One sense of 'practical' is closely related to 'relevant' as set out above: mathematics as serving a practical purpose in life. However another dominant sense of the use of 'practical' was as some sort of embodiment. Many of the examples elicited suggested teachers took a piece of mathematical content and then found some means of making it practical by embodying it, either within physical materials, diagrams or within some 'real-world' context. In this interpretation, practical is closer to being a teaching style or learning aid than the applying of mathematics to solve problems. Examples of practical-as-embodiment included: using tape measures to find numbers; using pebbles for sorting; asking children what position they are in when lining up; and drawing fraction 'cakes'. Teachers with this interpretation of practical work reported high percentages of time spent on UAM. This reception teacher indicated more than 80 per cent of her mathematics time involved using and applying:

> Using maths in everything, yes. I mean we have a brick, a plastic brick for each child and I divide the whole class into four teams . . . so each child has got a plastic brick and they're in four colour sets and then when somebody is away we put the plastic brick on the side, so we've got a very visual, very large-scale representation of who's here and who isn't.

As the focus in practical-as-embodiment was on developing some mathematical content understanding, usually either in terms of measuring or counting, there was little sense that the teachers regarded it as necessary or desirable for the pupils to perceive a purpose to the tasks. This example from a Yr2 teacher is typical. Asked to recall an example of a recent activity which involved the children in using and applying their maths, the teacher replied:

> Um, not recently, but off the top of my head, they had to measure a variety of parts of their body and record the answers. They were given a tape measure . . . and asked for circumferences round their head and foot sizes and shoes and they just had to go away and record their answers.

Teachers talked of allowing pupils to find their own methods for practical activities but there was little evidence that the methods used were discussed or elaborated upon. Overall the impression was one of physical activity assumed to lead to mathematical thinking without overtly exploring such thinking.
    Yr1 teacher:

> Using and applying maths, let's see, what they enjoy doing is measuring each other, they love measuring each other, or weighing each other or going round asking each other questions about how many people they've got in the family, or what sort of car they've got. They like doing that.

At KS1 there was a clear preference in the interviews for activities which were focused on practical activity. Half the examples offered involved measurement and most of the other examples arose out of some practical situation either set up by the teacher or through the day-to-day classroom events.
    Most of the KS2 teachers interviewed also gave examples which were practically orientated, either because of the nature of the mathematics involved (particularly measuring), or because of the context (shopping or map making) or because of the outcome (models).

UAM as 'stand alone' investigations

KS3 teachers were most likely to be catering for UAM through mathematical investigations. The impact of GCSE coursework is significant here and interview teachers talked of having to begin investigations in earlier years. Such coursework is mainly focused on investigations and not often explicitly related to the other mathematics ATs except algebra. Any 'real-life' problems discussed were likely to be based around hypothetical situations without implemented solutions, for example designing a room. Again GCSE coursework was an influence: one teacher spoke about the difficulty of finding applications which had mathematical content at a sufficiently high level to satisfy moderators.

The examples offered by KS3 teachers were more balanced across the ATs but the emphasis on investigations biased the coverage towards Ma3 (algebra). Ten of the 20 examples provided could be classed as mathematical investigations and all of them might be expected to lead to an algebraic generalisation. Three of the 10 teachers cited surveys as examples of Ma1 and three provided similar modelling or hypothetical real-life problems – designing or decorating flats, kitchens or bathrooms – with potential for work on Ma4 (Shape and space). However the dominant approach to actually selecting activities seemed more to do with matching them to pupils' abilities than providing balance across the ATs.

A Yr7 teacher:

> Q: Your planning for [Ma1], how does that differ from what you're doing for the other bits?
> A: I have to think more about it myself. What I try and do is find an activity that will satisfy the group that I've got . . . that there is something that they can all achieve at least to start . . . but there is also room for the brighter ones to go on.

Two teachers spoke in terms of selecting investigations to support the content of Ma2–5 and one of these saw the link being in terms of assessment rather than developing understanding although the department had begun to think about how content aspects could also be reinforced.

A Yr9 teacher:

> What we envisage is that each, like, strand, each area of work will have one piece of work within it which could assess Ma1.
> [*Later*] I think recently we've begun to think that we're perhaps spending too much time on it [Ma1] and we have to be aware of, while they're doing these projects, we must sort of be reinforcing other skills, bringing them in, not have the sort of long-winded projects that they spend ages on and . . . given half a chance they'll start colouring things in, so it's a double lesson on colouring in. So we're aware that we have to bring the actual maths skills into our work on [Ma1].

IMPLEMENTING THE TEXTS OF UAM: EFFECTS OF TEACHERS' INTERPRETATIONS

Questionnaire data had indicated an apparently high degree of planning for UAM. However interview data presented a different picture with little evidence of specific planning for UAM. Where teachers indicated that they did plan for UAM their particular interpretation of the NC requirements often meant such planning was restricted. Only eight of the KS1 and 2 interview teachers indicated that they explicitly paid attention to UAM in their planning. This seemed in the main to focus on either topic work or making provision for practical work.

A Yr2 teacher:

> Q: And how do you plan for them to use and apply their mathematics?
> A: I mean for example . . . the shop . . . I actually set up the toy shop myself, then this . . . the shop that they've just done here . . . I actually let them go about designing it and doing it themselves . . . so it might not be to the standard that I probably would have done it, but it's their own work, and they used their own knowledge to well, to draw on from what I gave to help.

A Yr6 teacher described what she perceived as planning for context and strategy for Ma1:

> Q: Right, how do you . . . or do you actually plan for [Ma1] to happen?
> A: I plan for using within the maths lessons, that is very carefully . . . the applying . . . you have to plan for in your science and your geography, because you can't do it any other way. You have got to say, I am going to . . . now what maths are involved . . . who can do that maths, how do I prevent Robert taking over, because he is good at maths, how can I get the others involved . . . and we've come to an arrangement, Robert and I, he comes and whispers the answer to me . . . waiting for the others to come up with it, this sort of tactic. So you have to plan.

The picture of planning for Ma1 at KS3 was unclear, with few clear-cut statements from interviewees. Several KS3 teachers expressed the opinion that their planning for Ma1 had not been adequate in the past, and they were beginning to focus more on this now, and write Ma1 into the planning. The requirement to assess Ma1 seemed to have increased the pressure to focus on this area. There were indications that teachers were researching more open-ended activities. Where explicit provision was expressed as being made for Ma1 it appeared to be mainly through the provision of additional 'bolt-on' investigations. Five of the 10 teachers interviewed spoke in terms of 'banks' of investigations often organised for year groups. At one extreme these were only implemented intermittently, 'the odd whole-class investigation' (Yr8 teacher). Other departments had introduced requirements to do a set number of investigations – for example, 12 per year or one per half-term.

A Yr8 teacher described how the department had modularised the mathematics curriculum and were building investigative activities into each module:

Well hopefully it will do a number of things, it will pull together the work, give it some kind of vehicle to be extended, like if you've done a piece of work say on area or perimeter, where you've just gone through the basics, which you've got to do every now and then, it will actually give an avenue where that can then go on further. You can find out something more, perhaps have more appreciation of the particular relationships between [things].

The majority of teachers at all key stages spoke in terms which suggested that it was not necessary to plan for UAM. The general impression was that either Ma1 was inseparable from all teaching of mathematics or was dealt with in an opportunistic manner. In either case, specific planning was not necessary.

A Yr2 teacher:

I don't sit down and think, oh I'd better do that because they might use it and apply it somewhere else, and to me, using and applying maths, actually, some of it is just, it's got to be done naturally rather than having to sit down and be planned for them.

A Yr6 teacher:

Q: Yes, and do you plan for [UAM]?
A: Um . . . not specifically, no. Although a lot of the activities that I do actually do include [Ma1] . . . by nature of the activities that I do. I don't specifically say right, I've got to cover [Ma1] here . . . and so on, but it's usually incorporated in the activity. And again . . . I'm sort of naturally doing it as I go along.

A Yr4 teacher:

Q: Do you plan at all for [UAM] specifically?
A: No, no . . . not . . . certainly not . . . one [Ma1] . . . I'm more just sort of missing one, and saying right . . . that's virtually everything that's coming along is going to be partly one, isn't it?

A Yr5 teacher:

Q: Do you actually put it [UAM] into your plans at the moment?
A: It's a good question, I have to be honest, I mean, . . . I probably don't directly, no . . . I think I tend to hope that I cover it on the way.

For another Yr5 teacher the mismatch between her beliefs about what constituted using and applying mathematics and her reading of UAM was so great that it had led her to dismiss the AT almost completely:

Q: Yes, and when you're planning, do you actually look at [Ma1] to put into your plans?
A: Well I do look at [it] and each time I look . . . I think . . . well I really ought to include these, and I come up against this sort of feeling that . . . they don't work.
[*Later*] Well actually I felt that I was doing a lot better before [Ma1] came along, because, I would always try and relate whatever topic was being done, like number work or something, back to a practical outcome, . . . like shopping lists were a favourite of mine and, I don't know, paying for things and working [out] how

many of so much [costs] and somehow this is lost in [AT1]. I mean maybe it's just my perception of it but somehow I don't feel that what they've put in there has any particular relevance to real life.

Taken to its extreme, the mismatch between personal belief and the Order may make it impossible to implement Ma1 or at least to assess it within the mathematics class.

A Yr8 teacher:

I don't agree in total at all with the National Curriculum people in the way they are approaching using and applying mathematics. I don't agree with their methods of assessment of using and applying mathematics, I think they've totally got that wrong ... What I would want is to pass the using and applying mathematics to every department in the school, get them to say yes. I mean in this year group this particular topic, we are covering that section of work and they would say where the mathematics is being used and applied and we would use their evidence or they would supply the evidence that a particular topic has been covered in making that particular model or doing that particular piece of science or geography, ratio, scales, it's done in geography, that's where you find the application of it and that's where it should be.

On the other hand, if teachers are prepared to question their own practices and beliefs, the changes precipitated could be marked. This Yr2 teacher described how previously she had covered things in 'little units' aimed largely at individuals, but the challenges presented by Ma1 and its associated assessment had brought about changes:

Talking in groups more, over things, and letting them come up with their own ideas and then letting them carry on, and then setting things up which they can ... I would do the tasks and set them at different levels to start it, [now] it's finding tasks that they can work within levels ... [*Later*] I'm not there but at least I know where I'm supposed to be going.

However, such responses were very much the exception.

DISCUSSION

Top-down models of curriculum development rest on certain assumptions. In particular, as Codd (1988) argues, they rely on a 'technical-empiricist' view of policy-making. Such a view is associated with an idealist perception of language as a transparent carrier of ideas and meanings. This in turn results in the 'intentional fallacy' (*ibid.*) – the assumption that any reading of the texts will correspond to the authors' intentions. On the basis of these interviews it would seem that as far as UAM was concerned the wording of the documentation may have had unintended consequences.

From the NC texts it is not difficult to see how a view that UAM is primarily to do with everyday applications may arise. At Levels 1, 2 and 3 of AT1 (1989 Order) eight out of the nine examples involve measurement in some form. The focus on logical reasoning is difficult to reconcile with the title 'Using and Applying Mathematics' as this hardly conveys a sense of the purely mathematical. Indeed, the title may be read as something of a tautology. In everyday usage the distinction between using something and applying it is not clear and there is little in the body of the AT which exemplifies this.

Accompanying the Order was NSG and it is in this guidance that possible interpretations of Ma1 are fleshed out, although as these were written after the development of the curriculum, and by a group of authors different from the curriculum writers, they rather represent a *post hoc* construction of intentions. The NSG argues that this part of the curriculum is about using mathematics, communicating in mathematics and developing ideas of argument and proof. The NSG also emphasises the two-way relationship between Ma1 and the other ATs (covering number, algebra, shape and space, and data handling) – the former motivating and requiring the latter, which in turn facilitate and enable the using and applying of mathematics. The model proposed is one of permeation: Ma1 and its PoS should 'permeate all other work in mathematics, providing both the means to, and the rationale for, the progressive development of knowledge, skills and understanding in mathematics' (DES/WO, 1989b, p. D3). While some examples of 'opening up' closed tasks are provided, bringing to the texts a belief that mathematical content can be developed through problem-solving might help make sense of what a permeation model of UAM might look like. But without that pre-existing understanding, there is little to support the development of it.

As indicated above, the supporting NSG goes some way towards clarifying the intentions behind Ma1 but evidence from both the questionnaire and interviews suggested that many teachers had devoted little, if any, time to studying this part of the documentation. In some cases it appeared that the details of Ma1 had been given scant, if any, attention by the teachers, a response no doubt encouraged by the popular view that UAM did not have 'proper' levels of attainment like the other ATs. It seemed that many teachers paid most attention to the title of Ma1, 'Using and Applying Mathematics', assuming the AT to be about real-world applications only. As discussed, the difficulty is that the title does not fully relate to the content of the assessment and teaching schedules, making some teachers feel frustrated or confused and further promoting a sense that Ma1 is unworkable.

Those closely involved in mathematics education may read the texts associated with Ma1 in ways that make it serve at least two purposes: first, UAM as a way to develop the understanding and linking together of different aspects of mathematical content; and, secondly, UAM can be seen as aiming towards developing pupils' more general mathematical problem-solving abilities including an understanding of, and the ability to engage in, reasoning, logic and proof, the processes of mathematical argument and justification. Articles supporting such interpretations have appeared, and continue to appear, in the professional journals.

However, such readings are more likely to arise from what mathematics educators bring to the texts than the content of the texts themselves. The mathematics education community must guard against the 'genetic fallacy' (Apple, 1992) arising out of the assumption that the motives of policy producers will guarantee how the arguments will be used. Mathematics educators may be able to 'read' the policy documentation associated with UAM in ways consistent with approaches to teaching mathematics that they would like to promote. However it cannot be assumed that these readings correspond to those of most teachers.

CONCLUSION

For many teachers UAM may represent changes and additions to the traditional pedagogy and content of the mathematics curriculum. But if teachers are interpreting UAM by paying attention to only parts of the Order, the title of the AT in particular, then they may believe it possible to implement using and applying with minimal, if any, changes to existing practice. Rather than broadening the range of teaching and learning experiences for pupils in mathematics, current practices may not only remain unaltered but also actually be reinforced by the readings of the documentation that teachers make.

Although the NCC has brought out additional guidance to help in the interpretation and implementation of UAM (NCC, 1992), it is likely that teachers' existing interpretations will be quite robust and resistant to change. If teachers have developed an understanding of Ma1 based largely upon the title 'Using and Applying Mathematics' and not the content of the PoS or SoAs, then although the activities that they are engaging their pupils in may be worthy, Ma1 is only being partially implemented. Under such circumstances difficulties in the implementation of Ma1 may be 'hidden' from some teachers by their particular interpretation. By examining the differing interpretations that teachers may hold about Ma1 there is the potential for such beliefs to be challenged, extended or developed.

NOTE

1. At the time of starting this research the mathematics NC comprised 14 ATs with two, 1 and 9, devoted to using and applying mathematics. The wording of each of these was identical but examples referred to different aspects of the curriculum: number/algebra, and shape and space/data handling. Halfway through the two years of the project, ATs 1 and 9 were combined into one target Ma1. This involved some minor rewording and changing of examples but the essence was essentially the same and the associated PoS remained virtually unaltered.

6

RESEARCH, POLICY AND POLITICS: FRICTION AT THE INTERFACE

Margaret Brown and David C. Johnson
King's College London

This chapter carries forward the themes from Chapter 1 in considering some of the turmoil in education accompanied by further changes in government and government organisations: another new Minister of Education and NCC and SEAC become SCAA. The focus moves to the Dearing review in 1993, the final year of the Mathematics Evaluation Project, and in particular some consideration of the impact, if any, of the project on the review and subsequent work in mathematics – new draft Orders (SCAA, 1994) and the final Order (DfE, 1995). We have not attempted to be comprehensive in our coverage in these areas, but rather have attempted to identify points which we feel might serve as 'snapshots' to reflect the title of the chapter.

NATIONAL TURMOIL: 1991–94

Changes to national tests and the NC

When the contract for the evaluation of the mathematics NC was awarded in May 1991, there was already a sense of unrest in the educational system. The interviews which took place with teachers the following year as part of the project revealed the fact that many teachers felt deeply angry over the way they had been treated by the government. The opposition was not to a national curriculum as such; indeed almost all teachers supported the notion of a national curriculum. Nor were there serious objections to the form and content that the mathematics curriculum had taken. The opposition was mainly to the manner, and to the speed, of its imposition:

> If we're thinking back over the last couple of years . . . I mean, it was like being stuck in the middle of a forest, with absolutely no chance of seeing the wood for the trees . . . and to be honest, my staff and I were very . . . well not suicidal, not quite . . . because with every bit of work that you did, suddenly something was changing elsewhere . . . and it became a farce. (Year 8 teacher)

> I have found it difficult to make sense of so much of what's coming on us all at once. (Year 1 teacher)

> I'm shattered; I came into teaching from industry and I always thought that teachers were rather morbid and depressing . . . but . . . they certainly are now if they weren't ten years ago. (Year 7 teacher)
>
> (Askew *et al.*, 1993, pp. 70, 129–30)

Although the evaluation was funded by the NCC and therefore was asked not to touch upon matters of assessment which were properly the responsibility of SEAC, teachers found it difficult not to mention their opposition to the notion of league tables and to publicly reported national testing.

The first round of national tests at KS1 (age 7) took place in 1991, although it had been agreed that the results would not be published. The National Union of Teachers (NUT), meeting at Easter 1991, had decided to seek agreement from their members involved in primary schools to boycott the tests. However by the time they were contacted, heads and Yr2 teachers had mastered what they were expected to do, and had made elaborate plans to cope. They therefore voted against the boycott although many said privately that they would have supported it if they had been consulted earlier. In the event teachers found the extent and organisation of the testing extremely difficult to manage, and the exercise was completed only with considerable support from heads, from supply and other teachers, and from LEA officers. The tests themselves were generally praised for their educational quality, and most teachers admitted that they had learned something in the process (Gipps *et al.*, 1995). Nevertheless there was anger that a league table of LEAs was made public by the government, with the resulting tabloid 'finger-pointing' at the lowest-performing LEAs, in spite of the promise that no publication of results would occur on the first run.

As a result of well reported objections to the testing load on teachers at age 7, the relatively new Secretary of State, Kenneth Clarke, promised simplification for the following year. A wish to avoid a similar outcry at KS3 presumably motivated his decision to stop the extended classroom-based assessment at KS3 that was receiving large-scale trials that summer (Daugherty, 1995). Without waiting for the results of the trials, which were actually very positive, he cancelled the contracts, having decided that short written tests would be used instead (Brown, 1992b).

Thus early in his appointment as Secretary of State for Education, Kenneth Clarke made three changes of direction. Only the least radical of these, the simplification of the KS1 testing, was strictly necessary and was generally popular.

The change to short written tests at KS3, and the cancelling of contracts in all subjects with the London University Consortium for Assessment and Testing in Schools (CATS) was in retrospect an unwise move, since the test-writers, especially those in English, had high-ranking positions in subject associations and strong links with teacher unions. Some were, not surprisingly, later to play a central role in leading the opposition to the new tests.

Finally, as recorded in Chapter 1, the hasty and unnecessary decision taken early in 1991, only 18 months after implementation of the 1989 Orders, to revise the national curricula in mathematics and science caused much anger among teachers who had invested considerable time in becoming familiar with it and in designing records. For example, teachers in our survey commented:

> and now they've changed them . . . I've got to start again . . . what we need is time to absorb them and get them working before anyone flings a newly written one at us. (Year 2 teacher)
>
> they go and re-write the damn thing every six months or a year or whatever . . . causes tremendous problems and wastes a terrible amount of time and money. (Year 9 teacher)
>
> relating everything we taught . . . to the national curriculum . . . took us two and a half years, and then it all changed, so I've become a bit cynical since then. (Year 8 teacher)
>
> (Askew *et al.*, 1993, pp. 129–30)

A further blow to many teachers occurred in July 1991 when John Major announced in a speech to the Centre for Policy Studies, a leading New Right organisation, that because coursework in GCSE was clearly so unreliable, in future most subjects would be restricted to a maximum of 20 per cent. This decision, apparently taken on the spur of the moment and with no basis of evidence, reversed the previous policy of all Secretaries of State in the Conservative government, including Kenneth Baker.

Growing politicisation

Alongside these changes to curriculum and assessment, Kenneth Clarke in the summer of 1991 changed the leadership of each of the two institutions responsible respectively for the curriculum and assessment, appointing members of the New Right in their place. At SEAC Philip Halsey was replaced by Lord Griffiths, previously the head of the Central Policy Unit in 10 Downing Street, and the person who was thought to have been responsible for urging the NC and the other free-market aspects of the 1988 Act on Margaret Thatcher. The person appointed to replace Duncan Graham at the NCC was David Pascall, a

BP manager and also an ex-member of the Central Policy Unit. Unlike their predecessors, an ex-headteacher and an ex-chief education officer, neither had any previous experience of working in the school education system.

New members were also appointed by the Secretary of State to the Councils, with educationists being replaced by prominent members of the New Right. Since both the new Chairmen were appointed part time, new Chief Executives were also selected, both with politically acceptable credentials.

The effects of this politicisation were soon felt; the NCC issued documents about the induction of pupils into an absolutist moral culture, while SEAC decided to issue an anthology drawn from writers of the traditional canon as a basis for the new written tests in KS3 English. The NCC then devoted time to considering how to follow up the results of a report commissioned personally by the Secretary of State which recommended greater formality of teaching methods in primary education (Alexander, Rose and Woodhead, 1992).

In retrospect, it seems odd that these overtly right-wing moves were made by Kenneth Clarke, a politician who is generally regarded as being on the left of the Conservative Party. The only explanation seems to be a determination to remove the 'educational establishment', evidently feared as having regained control and subverting Conservative intentions (Lawton, 1994).

Kenneth Clarke's successor, John Patten, arrived in 1992 to find deep dissatisfaction in the schools, and appeared quite unable to handle it. He openly demonstrated solidarity with the New Right, and antagonised further almost all groups by his inept pronouncements and failures to compromise.

Revolt and compromise

The dissatisfaction in schools came from two sources: the first was primary teachers in KS2 where the NC was being gradually introduced, leading up to Yr6 in 1993–94. Teachers were struggling to make sure all subjects were covered, and were under pressure to keep detailed 'checklist' records and prepare for national tests in 1994.

The second source was secondary English teachers who were upset at the changes from coursework assessment to written tests in both GCSE and KS3 tests, and especially at the form and content of tests planned at KS3 for the first round of national testing in 1993. Mathematics and science teachers, while angry at the change in the Orders, were less dissatisfied with the type of tests trialled in 1992 for use in 1993, although they shared with other teachers the general resentment against the imposition of testing.

It was the National Association for the Teaching of English (NATE) who first discussed a boycott of the 1993 tests. Following on from this there was growing agreement in the teacher unions that a boycott was justified. This was particularly because of the fact that teachers felt disenfranchised, with the New Right in complete control and following their own reactionary agenda in the

NCC and SEAC, apparently dictating terms to the Secretary of State. Thus the unions, one by one, polled their members and finally acted together, almost without precedent, in agreeing, and then carrying out successfully, a national boycott of all testing in the summer of 1993.

Clearly the government had to resolve the situation. A perhaps unexpectedly useful decision had earlier been made by John Patten to replace the two key bodies created in the Education Act 1988, NCC and SEAC, from October 1993 with a single agency, the School Curriculum and Assessment Authority (SCAA). This fortuitously gave the opportunity to remove the two New Right Chairmen appointed by Kenneth Clarke and replace them with someone more acceptable to the teacher unions. After something of a search, the announcement was made in March 1993 that the impeccably neutral ex-civil servant, Sir Ron Dearing, had agreed to move from his post administering support for HE to lead the new authority.

In a further placatory move, attempting unsuccessfully to try to persuade the teacher unions to call off the boycott, John Patten announced a full review of the NC and its testing. The review, to be undertaken by Sir Ron, would examine the scope for 'slimming down' the curriculum, the 10-level grading scale, and the complexity of the testing and central administrative arrangements.

Further policy shifts to try to break the deadlock on testing came first in spring 1993, including the announcement that there would only be a pilot of KS2 in 1994, and then in the summer, with John Patten on sick leave, when the more pragmatic Minister of State, Baroness Blatch, took charge and agreed further compromises. There would be no publication of league tables at KS1 and 3, and publication at KS2 would be postponed for at least two years.

THE DEARING REVIEW: 1993

Sir Ron Dearing, starting immediately in May 1993 on his task of reconciliation, brought a much-needed change of climate to the education system. For once, the leader of the two government agencies (soon to become one) appeared genuinely to want to discover what teachers had to say, and to understand the problems before trying to find solutions. Because of the urgency of the situation he had clearly obtained *carte blanche* from the Secretary of State to proceed in whatever ways and at whatever cost might be needed.

His methods were to pledge that he would find a solution which was acceptable to teachers, and then to invite, by questionnaires and through the columns of *The Times Educational Supplement*, all teachers to send their views directly to him. Alongside this he participated, through SEAC and NCC, in a series of invited conferences around the country with headteachers and other teachers. He was also clearly meeting frequently with the leaders of the teacher unions and with officials at the Department for Education (DfE).

All this ensured the popularity of the movement and the trust of teachers. Because the disagreement was with teachers rather than educationists, and because of the suspicions of the Secretary of State about the subversive educational establishment, Sir Ron generally avoided contact with educationists. It is clear that he was concentrating his considerable diplomatic skills on achieving agreement with the teacher unions to call off the boycott, rather than on achieving any specific educational purposes. It was also clear that such an agreement would be much easier to achieve with the secondary-based National Association of Schoolmasters and Union of Women Teachers (NASUWT), for which the argument was concerned only with workload, rather than with the primary-dominated NUT who were at least equally concerned with the problematic question as to whether the curriculum and testing arrangements encouraged good educational practice.

The Dearing Interim Report (1993), published promptly in August, set out an agenda for further action. Not surprisingly this took the line that the curriculum must be 'slimmed down' to reduce the burden on teachers and to allow some time for teacher choice. Proposals were made to set up *ad hoc* committees of teachers, both at each key stage and for each subject, who would draft the new Orders. In the case of mathematics the group appointed contained one advisory teacher, one university mathematician and the remainder were classroom teachers. Thus no educationists, from universities, LEAs or other agencies, were included. However such groups were conscientiously consulted by professional officers from the newly combined authority.

The second issue in the interim report relevant to mathematics concerned the future of the 10-level structure. The main alternative was that proposed by the New Right of summative results being reported on a scale A–E as in GCSE on the basis of a common test based on each key-stage PoS. A decision on this was to be deferred to the final report.

Thirdly, to meet the contradictory requirements of the teacher unions, it was necessary in the interim report both to embrace teacher assessment in principle and to remove in practice any responsibility on teachers to carry it out. However, presumably at the insistence of the Secretary of State, there was no climbdown on the need for end-of-key-stage external tests.

The interim report was generally well received among teachers, if less enthusiastically among educationists. Hence in 1993, when the final report of the Mathematics Evaluation Project was actually published, the climate among the teaching profession was, thanks to Sir Ron, considerably more optimistic than it had been in 1991.

THE IMPACT OF THE MATHEMATICS EVALUATION PROJECT

As indicated in the previous section, the Dearing review worked to a very tight timetable beginning with the remit from the government on 7 April 1993, the interim report produced on 23 July, accepted by the government on 2 August, and the final report produced on 20 December 1993 (published in January 1994). How did the work of the Mathematics Evaluation Project fit into this timetable?

While the Mathematics Evaluation Project might well have represented a small component in the Dearing review as this was a comprehensive consideration of all ten NC subjects and the assessment arrangements for all four key stages and beyond, it is noted here that the government's (NCC's) investment in the evaluation exercise was substantial. Mathematics was one of the three core areas for which work was commissioned to evaluate implementation issues – the other two were English (Warwick University) and science (Liverpool University). The funding for mathematics alone was £357,500 and the work was undertaken and completed by a team of six experienced researchers (2.5 full-time equivalents as all but one worked part time on the research). Hence, one might expect the findings and recommendations from each of the three evaluation projects, English, mathematics and science, conducted during the period 1991–93, to play an important part in the review process.

Project inputs to the Dearing review

The evaluation projects were indeed invited to participate. The Mathematics Evaluation Project was invited to present its findings to Sir Ron at a seminar on 22 September 1993 – well after the presentation and acceptance of the Dearing Interim Report by the government and shortly after the project had submitted its final report to SCAA (August 1993). (As final publication of the mathematics report (Askew *et al.*, 1993) was in December 1993, about the same time as Sir Ron submitted his final report to the government, the timing for dissemination did not allow those outside the official groups, SCAA and the government, access to the results and recommendations to inform their own deliberations and inputs to the consultation, yet again another potentially useful report appearing 'after the fact'.)

While the project final report to SCAA appeared after the Dearing Interim Report, this is not to say that other project documentation was not available to Sir Ron and those in SCAA who were conducting the review. The evaluation project had submitted interim reports to NCC each six months (March 1992, September 1992 and March 1993) during the two-year period. These were not merely reports on progress as the project team was also asked to address particular current issues and concerns, e.g. 'manageability of the curriculum in primary schools', in terms of selected components in the data being collected. As indicated in Chapter 2, the project team took the position that the research questions/issues were in fact much broader than those proposed in the initial specification and, with approval from NCC, the research was designed to enable some flexibility in drawing upon the range of data sets, to address the research questions in the specification and others which might arise during the period of the research. In light of the many changes and issues which arose this decision did indeed prove to be fortuitous, both for the research team and NCC (now SCAA). On the other hand, designing research to be flexible in anticipation of issues which might emerge represented a difficult task.

One might assume that the interim reports were available to those involved in the Dearing consultation. However, the moving of boxes of documents from York back to London (NCC and SEAC to new SCAA offices) meant that the probability or possibility of access to, and use of, these documents would seem to have been very low at best.

There was another important factor relevant to a consideration of project input to the consultation. It was also the case that an NCC subject officer, Peter Lacey, played an integral part in all phases of the research – participating in project meetings as a valuable and respected member of the research team and also acting as liaison between the project and other NCC officials. Peter also carried on with his post in the new organisation, SCAA, and hence he and others familiar with the interim reports and the activities of the evaluation were in a position to provide input from the project's reports and deliberations.

With the above said, however, the timing of the seminar presentation would seem to suggest that the major role of this input from the research team was to be more one of confirmation of current thinking, which was well along by this time, rather than presenting new inputs or raising new issues.

The seminar provided an opportunity both to present the research findings – reorganised to address the main issues in the Dearing review: slimming down the curriculum, the 10-level scale, testing arrangements, and advice to SCAA – and to discuss these with Sir Ron and other officials. (Note is again made here that the four themes in the Dearing review were quite different from the areas delineated in the initial specification to the project in 1991.) The 17 project Recommendations were grouped to address each of the four Dearing themes (see Chapter 2) and this represented the verbal/visual portion of the seminar presentation. A summary briefing paper which drew upon aspects of the research data deemed relevant to each of the four themes was also submitted to SCAA/Sir Ron prior to the seminar (see Appendix 3).

Successes and failures

The project's Recommendations (Chapter 2) and submission (Appendix 3) were specific to mathematics (and to KS1, 2 and 3) with some aspects relevant to the general aims of the review and others more directly concerned with future work related to the mathematics Order. Hence, it is difficult to ascertain which project findings/Recommendations might have had some impact on the review. In cases where review outcomes were consistent with project Recommendations (e.g. retain the 10-level scale – Recommendation

2) it would appear to have been the case that this was consistent with inputs from many other sources across the range of school subjects (teachers and school administrators and professional associations), and as such merely added to the support obtained through the consultation. It is much easier to identify those outcomes for which the project Recommendations or advice was ignored or rejected in terms of some other conflicting evidence or beliefs (the latter is included here as certain aspects of the review seemed to come from government expectations, i.e. outcomes which were almost required in terms of the 'turmoil' of the period). Highly visible items here are project Recommendations 1 and 3: 'Retain the statutory mathematics Order in place, without any slimming down, until teachers of all year groups have had a sufficiently long period working with it to fully articulate its strengths and weaknesses' and 'Allocate a period for extensive development, trialling and evaluation for any proposed changes to the statutory Order, before they can pass into law'. These were included under the Dearing themes of 'slimming the curriculum' and 'advice to SCAA' ('time and process' in Chapter 2). Support for these project Recommendations came from a range of data sources, with that most directly relevant being the professional development aspects of the teachers who participated in Study 2, sequencing and progression – see Chapter 4. It was also clear from Study 4, planning, that 'time was needed for teachers to take on some feeling of *ownership* of the curriculum' (see Chapters 2 and 3) and that the full implementation of 'Using and Applying Mathematics' (UAM) was likely to be an ongoing and lengthy process (see Chapter 5).

Time apparently was not really on the agenda as the 'big bang' approach was clearly that which was favoured at the time of the project seminar and (in our opinion) we had little influence on the result of the consultation. So one outcome from the Dearing Final Report was to be a new mathematics Order, the third within six years, in place for implementation in August 1995, eight months after the Dearing Final Report was published.

Two other important areas in the project's Recommendations which one might feel would warrant some consideration as they had implications beyond mathematics were those of 'resources' (Recommendations 9 and 15) and IT (Recommendation 13). Recommendation 9, 'Encourage more resources in terms of cover and/or advisory support to be given to schools for whole-school or departmental planning of schemes of work in mathematics, and development and/or selection of learning activities' and 15, 'Encourage reversal of the present trend of decrease in resource provision for mathematics advisory and support staff, at school, LEA and national levels, and in Higher Education', were put forth as an indication of teachers' perceptions that people support was more important than more documents to read – a phenomenon of the times, and likely to continue even though the audience may be becoming tired of 'yet another epistle from SCAA' which they don't have time to read.

Recommendation 13, in regard to IT, was that the government/SCAA

Give more attention to policy for IT use and development at all levels, school, LEA and national, which includes providing additional guidance to teachers, increasing the level of support provided by advisory staff both within and across schools and increasing the provision of IT resources, enabling easy access by pupils and teachers.

Hence this Recommendation embodied support, as indicated above, as well as having implications for curriculum.

IT, computers, was addressed by the teacher groups in Study 2 (see Chapter 4) and concern was also expressed by the first Mathematics Working Group (Chapter 1). Yet little attention was given to this crucial area in the Dearing Final Report (1994, p. 29) – there is a reference to the idea that the 'basics of information technology should be regarded as a core skill' and that 'these comments [views expressed during the consultation] are well-founded and . . . they should be taken up in the work that lies ahead' (*ibid.*, p. 30). However, such statements provide little guidance as to the integration of IT in subjects, beyond the fact that this was to be left to the next phase when new Orders were to be developed, i.e. left to subject working groups to delineate what needed to be done. There was a potential tension for mathematics as the exercise was about 'slimming the curriculum' and the review also indicated that the content was to remain basically the same – 'It will not involve the introduction of new material' (*ibid.*, p. 35) and 'I have recommended minimum change to the core subjects' (*ibid.*, p. 73).

The new mathematics Order

The new mathematics Order (draft, SCAA, 1994; final, DfE, 1995) is now in place – published in January 1995 for implementation at KS1, 2 and 3 in August 1995 and at KS4 in August 1996–97, Yr10 and 11 respectively. However, KS4 is now described to be consistent with the usual GCSE as administered by examination boards with letter grades – levels within ATs end with KS3.

While it is not intended in this book to examine the 1995 Order in detail, there are aspects of the new document (and the 1994 draft document) which suggest that the Mathematics Evaluation Project did have some impact. First, is the fact that the 1995 Order has in fact been developed around a key-staged PoS. Project Recommendation 4 was

Start as soon as possible to work with groups of teachers to design and trial a key-staged document to form a basis for teachers' planning, relating to current SoAs . . . start[ing] as a non-statutory document, with the likelihood of parts of it becoming a new statutory programme of study after appropriate and rigorous trialling.

It is clear from the time-line that substantial aspects of this Recommendation could not be included in the development of the 1995 Order. However, there was some important information included in the project report (Askew *et al.*, 1993) to aid in the task – in particular the work of the teacher groups in Study 2 (see Chapter 4) and to a lesser extent the questionnaire and interview results for Study 4, planning, and Study 1, difficulties (see Chapters 2 and 3 in Askew *et al.*, 1993, and Chapter 3 in this book).

It was also the case that the preparation of the new Order was undertaken by SCAA as an 'in-house' task (the external *ad hoc* Consultative Committee mainly performing the function of reviewing successive documents), and two subject officers, Peter Lacey and Angela Walsh, with considerable experience of the Mathematics Evaluation Project took on important roles. As indicated previously, Peter was the NCC subject officer linked to the Mathematics Evaluation Project, and Angela was in fact a member of the evaluation project research team and one of the two researchers co-ordinating the work of the teacher groups. Hence, both Peter and Angela were in a position to draw on the experience of the research and in particular the deliberations of the teachers who participated in Study 2. This does not excuse the fact that no trialling took place, but under the circumstances it would appear that the work of the project was utilised in as much as it was feasible to do so. On the other hand, important issues related to such areas as differentiation and cross-curricular work (and the need for advice to publishers in these and other areas) remain – see Chapter 3. While work on these topics should draw upon the good ideas of practitioners, they most certainly will also require 'appropriate and rigorous trialling'. It is accepted here that such work may well go beyond that which would be included in a statutory Order and it is anticipated that this will quite appropriately represent future work in SCAA.

A second feature in the 1995 Order is the fact that Ma1, 'Using and Applying Mathematics' (UAM), has been retained as a separate AT – but not without considerable debate. The presence of this AT is prominent in the PoS and the level descriptions (with some simplification of the wording in each). Aspects of the Mathematics Evaluation Project Recommendations related to this AT were to 'Ensure in the assessment Order for each key stage . . . that at least in some parts of the tests, assessment of Ma1 is integrated with that of other attainment targets' (Recommendation 6) and that priority should be awarded to UAM 'for the provision of support to teachers . . . includ[ing] extensive extended Inset, further exemplar materials, advice to publishers, and stimulus for in-school reflection and development . . . [and the] commissioning [of] work to study and report on successful collaborative whole school planning relating to [UAM]' (Recommendation 8). These grew out of the issues and problems identified by the evaluation project, not the least of which were teachers' interpretations of the meanings of the AT (see Chapters 2 and 5; Askew *et al.*, 1993, Chapter 5).

The most controversial aspect of the consultation in the initial stages of developing the new mathematics Order was whether or not the process aspect of UAM (Ma1) should be integrated into the other ATs – and there would no longer be a separate target. The arguments here were that this would then become part of the teaching in the other areas, rather than being taught separately (as has been documented to be the more standard phenomenon). This alternative was set out as an appendix to the main draft mathematics Order (SCAA, 1994) – however, this was strongly opposed by the leading mathematics organisations – for example, the Joint Mathematical Council (JMC) noted that such integration 'would lead to too much concentration on techniques to the detriment of practice in applying techniques and solving problems' (Hofkins, 1994, p. iii). While the Mathematics Evaluation Project looked specifically at promising practice in integrating this AT with the other targets (as supported in the NSG which accompanied the 1989 Order), it was also clear that there was still much work to be done before this would become common practice. Hence the retaining of the separate AT was deemed important and desirable, but with SCAA taking responsibility for supporting further activity in this area. Thus it remains to be seen what steps will be taken in the coming years.

One final observation in regard to the 1995 mathematics Order – this is that of the place of IT tools and (mathematically related) concepts in school mathematics. As noted above a key feature in the new Order is that of the presentation of a key-staged PoS, and this is prefaced in 'Common Requirements' with six (really three) bullet points, the third of which is 'Information Technology': 'Pupils should be given opportunities where appropriate, to develop and apply their information technology (IT) capability in their study of mathematics' (DfE, 1995, p. 1). The relative balance of references to IT in the PoS, when contrasted with the 1989 or 1991 Order, has been increased with some reference to the 'use' of computers or computer software in ATs 2–4; but little if any in Ma1, except to the extent one would interpret the phrase 'select and use the appropriate mathematics or mathematics equipment or materials' to incorporate the selection and use of IT; and no reference at all appears in KS4 'Further Material' (*ibid.*, pp. 20–21). The Mathematics Evaluation Project team's concern here is again one of future support as suggested in their findings and Recommendations.

In light of the above, it would appear that the 1995 mathematics Order was mainly a cosmetic slimming down of the previous version with minor corrections and new, but not overly helpful, PoS for each key stage. One might ask whether the comment of a Yr6 teacher, when interviewed about the change from the 1989 to the 1991 mathematics Order, might not still be relevant:

> I can't see that . . . well, from the point of view that you've got less attainment targets to deal with . . . and . . . your records can be small . . . but I'm not sure that they're really that much different because . . . as far as I can see they're really the same things, but just sort of squashed down. So you've still got to cover the same stuff. It's almost like a sort of con trick, to try and make people think that it's less than it really is.
>
> (Askew *et al.*, 1993, p. 129)

THE YEARS 1995–2000

One recommendation in the Dearing Final Report (1994, p. 9) was that 'no further major changes should be made to the National Curriculum Orders for five years following the review'. As the 'Government accept[ed] in full the main recommendations' (DfE, 1993) this should mean that the opportunity will be there to study, reflect and evaluate, in preparation for the next review – but this requires forward planning! What is the likelihood of such foresight? Where will we be in 1999 or the year 2000 when the government is almost certain to feel the need to rush ahead yet again?

Proper research takes time; one might suggest that it would take a minimum of two or three years to conduct field work designed to address significant issues, many of which are known now and some easily linked to the outcomes of the evaluation reported in this book. Will research have some role to play in the next review process? Will the potential inputs from such work be taken into account in the timing of events? If so it would seem that consideration needs to be given now to defining a research and evaluation *programme* to begin in 1996, or no later than 1997. For mathematics this should also take into consideration work already being undertaken, i.e. research 'currently' supported by the Economic and Social Research Council (ESRC) as well as those projects funded by charitable foundations and government agencies, e.g. the Teacher Training Agency (TTA) commissioned research on 'effective teachers of numeracy', and personal efforts as indicated in the research proceedings of, for example, the British Society for Research on Learning Mathematics (BSRLM), the British Congress for Mathematics Education (BCME) and the British Educational Research Association (BERA).

Unfortunately it would appear that the real world of politics and policy for (mathematics) education continues to suffer from an 'I've been through it and hence know what is important' (so why do we need research?) and a strong element of distrust of the 'education establishment and their trendy ideas'. Will future government ministers and their advisory groups react differently? The next five to ten years of the mathematics NC in England and Wales should indeed prove to be interesting ones.

APPENDIX 1

**NCC Maths
Evaluation Project**

Code No.

Evaluation

of the

National Curriculum

in Mathematics

at

Key Stages 1, 2 and 3

Questionnaire for teachers

Part 1

Please return both parts of the completed Questionnaire in the stamped envelope provided by December 16th, 1991.

If you have any queries, please contact Alison Millett, Project Officer, Maths Evaluation Project, CES Kings College, Cornwall House Annex, Waterloo Road, London SE1 8TX.   Telephone 071.872.3081.

The following abbreviations will be used throughout the questionnaire:

ATs	– Attainment Targets*	SoAs	– Statements of Attainment*
PoS	– Programmes of Study,	NSG	– Non-Statutory Guidance
UAM	– Using and Applying Mathematics	Num	– Number
Alg	– Algebra	Sh & Sp	– Shape and Space
Hand. data	– Handling data	Prob	– Probability
NC	– National Curriculum	Meas	– Measures

* See below

Mathematics Attainment Targets

AT1   Use number, algebra and measures in practical tasks, in real-life problems and to investigate within mathematics itself

AT2   Understand number and number notation

AT3   Understand number operations (addition, subtraction, multiplication and division) and make use of appropriate methods of calculation

AT4   Estimate and approximate in number

AT5   Recognise and use patterns, relationships and sequences and make generalisations

AT6   Recognise and use functions, formulae, equations and inequalities

AT7   Use graphical representation of algebraic functions

AT8   Estimate and measure quantities and appreciate the approximate nature of measurement

AT9   Use shape and space and handle data in practical tasks, in real-life problems and to investigate within mathematics itself

AT10   Recognise and use the properties of two dimensional and three dimensional shapes

AT11   Recognise location and use transformations in the study of space

AT12   Collect, record and process data

AT13   Represent and interpret data

AT14   Understand, estimate and calculate probabilities

Example of Statement of Attainment (SoA)

From AT 10, Level 3.
sort 2-D and 3D shapes in different ways and give reasons for each method of sorting.

Questionnaire for teachers at key stages 1, 2 and 3

Please read the following notes before you begin

We realise that teachers are at very different stages in implementing the National Curriculum.   You may find some of the questions quite difficult to complete, but please do your best and be as honest as you can.   It is important to get a true picture of the situation throughout the country.

The questionnaire has been produced in two booklets.   This has been done as the questionnaire is quite long and you may wish to complete it in two sessions. Each booklet should take between 30 and 45 minutes.   Both parts are equally important.

Please tick in the appropriate boxes, or ring the answer, as necessary.

Background information - about your school

Size of school – number of pupils

0-99 ❑   100-249 ❑   250-499 ❑   500-749 ❑   750-1200 ❑   over 1200 ❑

Type of school

Infant/First ❑   Junior ❑   Primary/Combined ❑   Middle ❑
Secondary: 11-16 ❑   12-16 ❑   11-18 ❑   12-18 ❑   13-18 ❑

Other school characteristics [tick all that apply]:

County ❑   Voluntary aided/controlled ❑
Selective ❑   Non-selective ❑
Inner City ❑   Other Urban ❑   Suburban ❑   Rural ❑

Classes (for mathematics) are organised
[Please tick any of the following statements which apply to key stages 1, 2 or 3 in your school]

strictly by year group and mixed ability   ❑
vertically grouped and mixed ability   ❑
mixed ability with higher attaining children with an older year group   ❑
generally mixed ability but with some setting (eg higher attainers)   ❑
setting for maths   ❑
broad banding or streaming for all subjects   ❑

Organising your mathematics teaching.

The last digit of the Code Number at the top right-hand corner of the cover of this questionnaire refers to a particular year group. Please answer **questions 1 and 2** with reference to *one* class containing pupils in this year group.

1. **When teaching mathematics, for what proportion of the time do you organise this class in the following ways?**

	<5%	5%-20%	21%-50%	51%-80%	>80%
whole class	❏	❏	❏	❏	❏
ability/attainment groups	❏	❏	❏	❏	❏
mixed ability groups (teacher chosen)	❏	❏	❏	❏	❏
friendship groups (pupil chosen)	❏	❏	❏	❏	❏
individuals	❏	❏	❏	❏	❏
other.	❏	❏	❏	❏	❏

2. **Which of the following most closely describes how you allocate work to children in this class? [You may tick more than one.]**

same work, same pace	❏
same work, different pace	❏
same work but at different times	❏
same maths topic, different work	❏
different maths topic, different work	❏
same starting points, different outcomes	❏
other.	❏

Planning your mathematics teaching

3. **Who do you plan with?**

	yearly	termly	half-termly	weekly	daily	never
on your own	❏	❏	❏	❏	❏	❏
with year group teachers	❏	❏	❏	❏	❏	❏
with one or two other teachers	❏	❏	❏	❏	❏	❏
with the post holder/HOD	❏	❏	❏	❏	❏	❏
with the whole staff /maths dept	❏	❏	❏	❏	❏	❏
with staff from other schools	❏	❏	❏	❏	❏	❏

4. **Please indicate how often you plan for these various sets of pupils.**

	yearly	termly	half-termly	weekly	daily	never
key stage group	❏	❏	❏	❏	❏	❏
year group	❏	❏	❏	❏	❏	❏
whole class	❏	❏	❏	❏	❏	❏
groups of pupils	❏	❏	❏	❏	❏	❏
a few individuals	❏	❏	❏	❏	❏	❏
everyone individually	❏	❏	❏	❏	❏	❏

5. **Please indicate which documents you use for planning, and how often you use them.**

	yearly	termly	half-termly	weekly	daily	never
NC documents	❑	❑	❑	❑	❑	❑
LEA material	❑	❑	❑	❑	❑	❑
HMI material	❑	❑	❑	❑	❑	❑
teachers' handbooks (commercial schemes)	❑	❑	❑	❑	❑	❑
pupils' books (commercial schemes)	❑	❑	❑	❑	❑	❑
materials developed in school	❑	❑	❑	❑	❑	❑
magazines and periodicals	❑	❑	❑	❑	❑	❑
other	❑	❑	❑	❑	❑	❑

Using the National Curriculum documents

Note – please refer to the Orders in place in 91-92, ie those issued to schools in 1989, NOT the new Orders.

6. **How often do you refer to each of the following areas of the National Curriculum documents in your planning?**

	yearly	termly	half-termly	weekly	daily	never
Statements of Attainment	❑	❑	❑	❑	❑	❑
Attainment Targets	❑	❑	❑	❑	❑	❑
Programmes of Study	❑	❑	❑	❑	❑	❑
Non Statutory Guidance	❑	❑	❑	❑	❑	❑
other	❑	❑	❑	❑	❑	❑

7. **Please indicate how your use of each of the following National Curriculum components has changed since a year ago.**

using	SoAs			ATs			PoS			NSG		
	more	same	less	more	same	less	more	same	less	more	same	less
	❑	❑	❑	❑	❑	❑	❑	❑	❑	❑	❑	❑

8. **Please indicate how useful you find each of the following in planning across a whole key stage.**   [Please ring the appropriate number.]

SoAs				ATs				PoS				NSG			
hi			lo	hi			lo	hi			lo	hi			lo
1	2	3	4	1	2	3	4	1	2	3	4	1	2	3	4

9. Please indicate to what extent you agree or disagree with each of these statements made by teachers about the *Programmes of Study.*

	agree		disagree
"They do not contain enough detail."	❑	❑	❑
"They have helped me to structure my planning effectively."	❑	❑	❑
"If would be better if they went across a whole Key Stage."	❑	❑	❑
"They should contain some of the general advice now in the NSG."	❑	❑	❑
"The lack of detail leaves me freer in my teaching."	❑	❑	❑
"They are no help at all as they are just a restatement of the SoAs."	❑	❑	❑
"Some examples of activities would help me to translate them into classroom practice."	❑	❑	❑

10. For your key stage, how well could you describe from memory what was in the different parts of the National Curriculum documents?

	well	quite well	a little	not at all
the ideas of each of the 14 ATs	❑	❑	❑	❑
the particular SoAs	❑	❑	❑	❑
the details of the PoS	❑	❑	❑	❑
the Non-Statutory Guidance	❑	❑	❑	❑

11. Do you have to plan for children with special needs?

Yes ❑   No ❑

If "Yes", please answer the next question.

12. How helpful do you find different parts of the NC documents in planning for children with special needs?

	very helpful	helpful	not very helpful
SoAs	❑	❑	❑
examples	❑	❑	❑
ATs	❑	❑	❑
PoS	❑	❑	❑
NSG	❑	❑	❑

13. **Do you have to plan for children for whom English is a second language?**

Yes ❑   No..❑

If "Yes", please answer the next question.

14. **How helpful do you find different parts of the National Curriculum documents in planning for children for whom English is a second language?**

	very helpful	helpful	not very helpful
SoAs	❑	❑	❑
examples	❑	❑	❑
ATs	❑	❑	❑
PoS	❑	❑	❑
NSG	❑	❑	❑

Using resources/classroom materials

Please answer the next two questions with respect to the same class as you referred to in questions 1 and 2.

15. **What proportion of mathematics work do most children in this class do from a commercial scheme?**

0% ❑   1%-5% ❑   6%-20% ❑   21%-50% ❑   51%-80% ❑   >80% ❑

16. **If you use a commercial scheme with this class, which of the following apply and how do you use them?**

	as the core of your work	as your main supplementary resource	as a range of material to draw from
Scottish Primary (SPMG)	❑	❑	❑
Ginn	❑	❑	❑
Peak	❑	❑	❑
Nuffield	❑	❑	❑
HBJ	❑	❑	❑
SMP 11-16	❑	❑	❑
SMILE	❑	❑	❑
KMP	❑	❑	❑
IMS	❑	❑	❑
SMG	❑	❑	❑
NMP	❑	❑	❑
other	❑	❑	❑

17. To what extent do you use the following when preparing classroom activities?

	a lot	a little	not at all
non-scheme mathematics books	❑	❑	❑
LEA produced material	❑	❑	❑
National Curriculum documents	❑	❑	❑
material produced in school	❑	❑	❑
ideas from other teachers	❑	❑	❑
your own ideas	❑	❑	❑

18. Please indicate which of the following resources have been acquired by your school since the introduction of the National Curriculum

New main scheme of texts   SPMG ❑   Ginn ❑   Peak ❑   Nuffield ❑
   HBJ ❑   SMP 11-16 ❑   SMILE ❑   KMP ❑   IMS ❑
   SMG ❑   NMP ❑   Other ❑

New supplementary materials for   Using and applying mathematics ❑
      Number and measures ❑
      Algebra ❑
      Shape and space ❑
      Handling data and probability ❑

Covering the Curriculum

19. Do your pupils in the year group identified do any mathematics as part of a cross-curricular project?

    Yes ❑   No ❑

If you answered "Yes" to question 19, please answer questions 20 and 21, otherwise, go on to question 22.

20. What proportion of the mathematics in your classroom is done:

	<5%	6%-20%	21%-50%	51%-80%	>80%
as a separate subject	❑	❑	❑	❑	❑
as part of a cross-curricular project	❑	❑	❑	❑	❑

21. How does each of the components in the National Curriculum in mathematics help you in planning through a cross-curricular approach? [Please ring the appropriate number.]

SoAs	ATs	PoS	NSG
hi lo	hi lo	hi lo	hi lo
1 2 3 4	1 2 3 4	1 2 3 4	1 2 3 4

22. When planning for coverage of the curriculum do you *mainly*

use information provided by the publisher of a scheme?   ❑
use your own/school scheme of work and check for any gaps?   ❑
other   ❑

Reviewing your work

23.   Which of the following describes how you ensure coverage as you go along? [Tick one box only]

use list provided by commercial scheme to know which ATs have been covered?   ❑
keep continuous record against the SoAs within ATs which have been covered?   ❑
keep a continuous record against PoS to show coverage?   ❑
some combination of the above   ❑
no record kept   ❑

24. Please indicate how you record NC coverage. [Tick all that apply]

For individuals ❑   for groups ❑   for the class ❑

25. How often do you review your plans with the intention of developing or changing them? [You may tick more than one].

daily   ❑
weekly   ❑
half termly   ❑
termly   ❑

26. What do you use to inform any review you make of your work? [You may tick more than one]

checklists of work covered   ❑
evidence of pupil attainment   ❑
Attainment Targets   ❑
Programmes of Study   ❑

Planning for everyone

The next question refers only to any pupils you teach who are agreed *by the school* to have special educational needs which significantly affect their mathematics.

27. For some or all of the pupils I teach: [Tick all that apply]

parts or all of the Maths NC are officially disapplied (not taught) ❑
completely different work has to be specially prepared ❑
work planned for the rest of the class has to be specially adapted ❑
no special work is prepared ❑

no such pupils ❑

28. Are there any students that you teach for whom English is a second language whose grasp of oral or written English affects their mathematical learning?

Yes, a few ❑
Yes, several ❑
Yes, the majority ❑
No , none ❑

Do you prepare work in a different form for some of these students? Yes ❑ No ❑

Using and applying mathematics (ATs 1 and 9)

29. What proportion of the time spent doing mathematics would you say is spent on work related to using and applying mathematics? (ATs 1 and 9)

<5% ❑   6%-20% ❑   21%-50% ❑   51%-80% ❑   >80% ❑

30. What would you say is the balance that you provide between real-life problems, practical work and mathematical investigations?

about the same of each ❑
mostly practical work,using equipment ❑
mostly real-life problems ❑
mostly mathematical investigations ❑

31. Which of the following describes how you plan for children to use and apply their mathematics? [Tick one only]

mainly through topics which are not exclusively mathematical ❑
mainly as part of the work on a mathematical topic(s) ❑
a balanced combination of the two above ❑

   and [Tick one only]

mainly through special activities eg GCSE coursework ❑
as part of all maths activities ❑

Thank you for completing Part 1 of the questionnaire
Please complete Part 2.

**NCC Maths
Evaluation Project**

Code No.

Evaluation

of the

National Curriculum

in Mathematics

at

Key Stages 1, 2 and 3

Questionnaire for teachers

Part 2

Please return both parts of the completed Questionnaire in the stamped
envelope provided by December 16th, 1991.

If you have any queries, please contact Alison Millett, Project Officer,
Maths Evaluation Project, CES Kings College, Cornwall House Annex,
Waterloo Road, London SE1 8TX.   Telephone 071.872.3081.

The following abbreviations will be used throughout the questionnaire:

ATs	– Attainment Targets*	SoAs	– Statements of Attainment*
PoS	– Programmes of Study,	NSG	– Non-Statutory Guidance
UAM	– Using and Applying Mathematics	Num	– Number
Alg	– Algebra	Sh & Sp	– Shape and Space
Hand. data	– Handling data	Prob	– Probability
NC	– National Curriculum	Meas	– Measures

* See below

Mathematics Attainment Targets

AT1   Use number, algebra and measures in practical tasks, in real-life problems and to investigate within mathematics itself

AT2   Understand number and number notation

AT3   Understand number operations (addition, subtraction, multiplication and division) and make use of appropriate methods of calculation

AT4   Estimate and approximate in number

AT5   Recognise and use patterns, relationships and sequences and make generalisations

AT6   Recognise and use functions, formulae, equations and inequalities

AT7   Use graphical representation of algebraic functions

AT8   Estimate and measure quantities and appreciate the approximate nature of measurement

AT9   Use shape and space and handle data in practical tasks, in real-life problems and to investigate within mathematics itself

AT10   Recognise and use the properties of two dimensional and three dimensional shapes

AT11   Recognise location and use transformations in the study of space

AT12   Collect, record and process data

AT13   Represent and interpret data

AT14   Understand, estimate and calculate probabilities

Example of Statement of Attainment (SoA)

From AT 10, Level 3.
sort 2-D and 3D shapes in different ways and give reasons for each method of sorting.

Areas of difficulty in implementing the National Curriculum in mathematics

32. Please indicate the NC attainment levels on which your teaching (in all classes) was focused last year. [Tick all that apply]

Level	1	2	3	4	5	6	7	8	9	10
	❑	❑	❑	❑	❑	❑	❑	❑	❑	❑

33. How would you classify your coverage of the Attainment Targets over the past year over the appropriate levels? [If you did not teach last year please omit this item]

You will find full titles of the Attainment Targets on the inside of the front cover of this booklet.

	covered well	just covered	not yet adequately covered	
AT1	❑	❑	❑	AT1
AT2	❑	❑	❑	AT2
AT3	❑	❑	❑	AT3
AT4	❑	❑	❑	AT4
AT5	❑	❑	❑	AT5
AT6	❑	❑	❑	AT6
AT7	❑	❑	❑	AT7
AT8	❑	❑	❑	AT8
AT9	❑	❑	❑	AT9
AT10	❑	❑	❑	AT10
AT11	❑	❑	❑	AT11
AT12	❑	❑	❑	AT12
AT13	❑	❑	❑	AT13
AT14	❑	❑	❑	AT14

34. Please indicate whether the following statements apply to the areas of mathematics given.

	UAM	Num	Meas	Alg	Sh & Sp	Hand.data	Prob
I have difficulty in implementing this area.	❑	❑	❑	❑	❑	❑	❑
My class does not work on this area every year.	❑	❑	❑	❑	❑	❑	❑
In most weeks my class works on this area.	❑	❑	❑	❑	❑	❑	❑
In most terms my class works on this area.	❑	❑	❑	❑	❑	❑	❑
I feel I should increase my coverage of this area.	❑	❑	❑	❑	❑	❑	❑
I would welcome INSET in this area.	❑	❑	❑	❑	❑	❑	❑

35. On the loose sheet enclosed you will find the detailed SoAs within one or two Attainment Targets. Please circle the levels in which you have had experience in teaching the National Curriculum. In the boxes, please tick SoAs which you have found difficult to implement.

36. Which of the following difficulties do you feel would apply to the areas of mathematics given?

	UAM	Num	Meas	Alg	Sh & Sp	Hand data	Prob
lack of previous experience of teaching this area of the curriculum	❑	❑	❑	❑	❑	❑	❑
lack of availabilty of suitable activities	❑	❑	❑	❑	❑	❑	❑
SoAs or PoS too difficult for pupils taught	❑	❑	❑	❑	❑	❑	❑
not easy to integrate into topic work	❑	❑	❑	❑	❑	❑	❑
not well covered by commercial scheme	❑	❑	❑	❑	❑	❑	❑
lack of clarity in the meaning of SoAs or PoS	❑	❑	❑	❑	❑	❑	❑
lack of confidence in own knowledge of area	❑	❑	❑	❑	❑	❑	❑
inadequate teaching materials	❑	❑	❑	❑	❑	❑	❑
classroom management and organisation a problem	❑	❑	❑	❑	❑	❑	❑
inadequate equipment	❑	❑	❑	❑	❑	❑	❑
requires change in teaching style	❑	❑	❑	❑	❑	❑	❑
difficulties in making provision for different levels of attainment	❑	❑	❑	❑	❑	❑	❑
sequencing of SoAs problematic	❑	❑	❑	❑	❑	❑	❑
too much to get through	❑	❑	❑	❑	❑	❑	❑
	UAM	Num	Meas	Alg	Sh & Sp	Hand data	Prob

37. Please indicate how helpful you have found or might find the following in implementing the National Curriculum in mathematics?

	found very helpful	found helpful	found not helpful	not available would be helpful	not available probably not helpful
INSET - in school	❑	❑	❑	❑	❑
INSET - out of school	❑	❑	❑	❑	❑
extra help in classroom	❑	❑	❑	❑	❑
more equipment/facilities	❑	❑	❑	❑	❑
books of ideas to accompany National Curriculum documents	❑	❑	❑	❑	❑
wider range in commercial schemes	❑	❑	❑	❑	❑
stronger role for NSG	❑	❑	❑	❑	❑
period of stability	❑	❑	❑	❑	❑
non-contact time	❑	❑	❑	❑	❑
LEA support	❑	❑	❑	❑	❑

38. Please indicate how useful you have found or might find the following kinds of in-service training and support activities for the NC Mathematics

	found very useful	found useful	found not very useful	not experienced would be useful	not experienced not useful
talks/workshops from advisers/advisory teachers/inspectors	❑	❑	❑	❑	❑
advisory teachers working in the classroom	❑	❑	❑	❑	❑
talks/course by lecturers from Higher Education Institute	❑	❑	❑	❑	❑
curriculum planning meetings and workshops with teachers from own school	❑	❑	❑	❑	❑
curriculum planning meetings and workshops with teachers from other schools	❑	❑	❑	❑	❑
advice, support, dissemination of information by coordinators/Deputy Heads/HODs	❑	❑	❑	❑	❑
workshops using distance learning/training packs	❑	❑	❑	❑	❑
other	❑	❑	❑	❑	❑

39. Please indicate how your approach to teaching mathematics over the past three years has changed for each of the following.   Also indicate whether or not this has been significantly influenced by the introduction of the National Curriculum.

	using more	using the same	using less	significantly influenced by NC Yes	No
practical work and/or apparatus	❏	❏	❏	❏	❏
problem solving	❏	❏	❏	❏	❏
investigations	❏	❏	❏	❏	❏
calculators	❏	❏	❏	❏	❏
computers	❏	❏	❏	❏	❏
pencil/paper calculation	❏	❏	❏	❏	❏
mental calculation	❏	❏	❏	❏	❏
cross-curricular work	❏	❏	❏	❏	❏
commercial schemes	❏	❏	❏	❏	❏
children working cooperatively	❏	❏	❏	❏	❏
children working competitively	❏	❏	❏	❏	❏
discussion between pupils	❏	❏	❏	❏	❏
discussion between yourself and pupils	❏	❏	❏	❏	❏
decision making by children	❏	❏	❏	❏	❏

Background Information   - About You

Female ❑   Male ❑

Years of teaching experience:
none(first year) ❑   1 ❑   2-5 ❑   5-10 ❑   more than 10 ❑

School/departmental responsibilities [Tick all that apply]:
   Head ❑   Deputy head ❑   HOD (secondary) ❑   2nd in Dept. (secondary)❑
   Maths coordinator (primary) ❑   Other allowance for Maths ❑

Year group(s) *you* **are teaching this year (1991/2) and taught last year (1990/91)**
[tick all boxes that apply]:

Year	Reception	Y1	Y2	Y3	Y4	Y5	Y6	Y7	Y8	Y9	Y10	Y11
1991/2	❑	❑	❑	❑	❑	❑	❑	❑	❑	❑	❑	❑
1990/91	❑	❑	❑	❑	❑	❑	❑	❑	❑	❑	❑	❑

Number of days of inservice training in mathematics *you* **had last year (1990/91)**
[tick all boxes that apply for each category]:

Number of days:		0	1	2	3	4	4-19	20 or more
Type:	School based	❑	❑	❑	❑	❑	❑	❑
	LEA based	❑	❑	❑	❑	❑	❑	❑
	Other site	❑	❑	❑	❑	❑	❑	❑

Please indicate if you studied maths as a main *academic* **subject in your:**

BEd ❑   BSc/BA ❑   Teachers Certificate ❑   'A'Level ❑

For secondary teachers only
Was 'teaching maths' a main focus in your teacher training (BEd/PGCE)?

                Yes ❑   No ❑

Indicate which, if any, of the following advanced professional study relating to mathematics or mathematics education you have undertaken [include current registration]:

Long course; 20 day INSET, OU module etc ❑   Diploma/Certificate ❑
Additional BA/BSc ❑   Masters Degree ❑

[please turn over]

In your school, do you have a:

permanent position? ❑   temporary position?❑
supply position?❑   part-time position?❑

In your school do you teach:
Only mathematics ?   ❑
Mainly mathematics?   ❑
All /most subjects in the curriculum?   ❑

The end of the questionnaire

Would you be willing to be interviewed during the second stage of this research?

Yes   ❑
No   ❑

If 'Yes', could you tell us your initials so that we may contact you again. This information will be entirely confidential to the research team, and will only be used for identification purposes.

Initials ....

Thank you very much for completing this questionnaire. We realise that it will have taken a long time, and we appreciate how busy you are. Your personal views on the implementation of the National Curriculum in mathematics will be very valuable to the continuing process of evaluating this major national initiative.

APPENDIX 2

NCC Maths Evaluation Project - Coding categories for Interview analysis: June 1992

Documents NC	D
Resources for teaching	R
Working with others	W
Timescale	T
Curriculum - including Activities, scheme, Content, Sequencing	C
Coverage - including Review	C v
Cross-Curricular topics	Cr
Pupil Organisation	PO
Teaching Strategies	T S
Differentiation	D f
Progression in learning	P
Difficulties /strengths- self	DcS
Difficulties /strengths- pupils	DcP
Difficulties/strengths - curriculum	DcC
Constraints/Influences - resourcing	CoR
Constraints/Influences - organisation	CoO
Constraints/Influences - outside	CoOu
Constraints/Influences - curriculum	CoC
Constraints/Influences - time	CoT
Constraints/Influences - assessment	CoA
UAM - Interpretation	UI
UAM - Strategies	U S
UAM - Resources	U R
Needs	N
Changes	Ch
Beliefs - maths	BM
Beliefs - pupils	B P
Beliefs - learning	BL

Note. These categories were extended further when it came to discussing specific issues or themes.

APPENDIX 3

Response to Sir Ronald Dearing from the NCC Maths Evaluation Project

The NCC Maths Evaluation Project, set up in 1991 to evaluate selected aspects of the implementation of the mathematics National Curriculum, has its research base in 3 HEIs (London, Cambridge and Birmingham). Data sources include three on-going working groups of teachers (total 24 teachers) and questionnaire and/or interview responses from 11 LEAs, 744 primary teachers and secondary maths teachers, and input from LEA advisers, HMIs and publishers.

The terms of reference of the research project did not directly focus on the four points identified for response. Information relating to all four points has resulted from the data collection, but in some cases it is based on the comments of a small number of teachers. Analysis and synthesis of data is in the final stages, and it is possible that some emphases may change during the writing up phase of the project. It should also be noted that, in this response, only the four questions identified have been addressed. The work of the project covers a considerably broader spectrum than this response would indicate.

1. Slimming Down the Curriculum?

Key Stage 3 The content of the curriculum itself was not perceived as a major problem at Key Stage 3.

Key Stage 2 teachers expressed most anxieties about extent of content, with, in all areas of mathematics, nearly a third of teachers indicating that there was too much to get through. These teachers were generally working with their perceptions of anticipated content to be covered, as the whole range of content had not been addressed at the time of the data collection. The National Curriculum is only just coming on stream for the whole of Key Stage 2. Initial findings from the project indicate potential problems particularly at Levels 4 and 5.

At **Key Stage 1**, concerns about manageability related to certain areas of the curriculum more than others, affecting nearly a third of teachers in those areas.

There were no clear indications, however, about what, if anything, teachers would wish to see lost; retaining breadth and balance in the mathematics curriculum was seen to be important, although several teachers indicated that their own priorities led them to spend more time on some areas, notably number. In some cases, the areas of mathematics in which teachers felt that there was too much to get through were also areas in which they experienced a variety of other difficulties, such as a lack of experience or subject knowledge, or inadequate resources, and there was some evidence to suggest that these difficulties might be ameliorated by, for example, the provision of suitable Inset or appropriate resources. There was no suggestion that Ma1 was not a valuable constituent of the mathematics curriculum; in fact in some cases, there was strong support for the importance of this component.

Teachers indicated that what they needed was time to digest and evaluate the complexity of the mathematics National Curriculum, without any more major changes being imposed on them. 60% of teachers across all key stages indicated that there was a need for a period of stability. Time to plan together and to develop schemes of work based on the National Curriculum could enable teachers to establish some degree of ownership over the curriculum, and the need to do this was viewed as important. The following quotations from teachers at Key Stage 1 and Key Stage 3 indicate the strength of feeling expressed by some teachers.

> '... what we need is time to absorb them [new Order] and get them working, before anybody flings a newly written one at us.

'Yes ... we're basically working ... with that [SCHEME text book], we're working with that, but we've also got the National Curriculum to work with as well, and of course bringing the two together, is another problem, particularly when they go and re-write the damn thing every six months or a year or whatever ... causes tremendous problems and wastes a terrible amount of time and money.'

While acknowledging teachers' perceived need for stability, it is possible to make suggestions for providing some assistance with reducing perceived curriculum overload which could be readily assimilated at the moment.

• moving to key stage programmes of study as in other subjects, ensuring that these allowed for considerable differentiation, ie following a 'topics to include which can be treated at different levels depending how far pupils have already got' rather than a 'content required to be covered by all' model; this suggestion represents one of the findings from groups of teachers working over the course of two years with the project.

• noting that one reason there appears to be too much for teachers to cover is that they insist on pupils following commercial schemes doggedly; if they were more selective in moving faster children through, they could more easily get to level 5 or 6 at the end of KS2; similarly they could afford to slow down with slower pupils who may not achieve beyond level 3 or 2 at the end of KS2 ie there appears to be too much to **teach**, but not necessarily too much to **learn**. Some teachers were beginning to look more critically at their schemes in an attempt to achieve greater differentiation in curricula.

• merging some ATs at lower levels or lower key stages eg Ma2, 3 and 5, **but not removing the content** . This would not require changes in the Order and could be accomplished by directing teachers to links within and across attainment targets. Further, this would remove the pressure on assessment, and, according to evidence collected from the teacher groups, would aid in rationalising the teaching.

• **retaining Ma1 as a separate attainment target**. Those teachers who were incorporating Ma1 into their planning appreciated a separate identity for Ma1 even though planning for its implementation through the other attainment targets.

• addressing some of the difficulties experienced by teachers in terms of the provision of Inservice training, or additional materials and resources.

• **demonstrating** to teachers where similar or complementary elements in other mathematics attainment targets or other subject areas might be taught in conjunction, thereby consolidating content, and **identifying** those elements. The Order as presented and the advice given tends to preclude the implementation of cross-curricular work which in itself helps to slim down the curriculum.

2. 10 levels?

The majority of interview teachers expressed positive views that the 10 level scale for statements of attainment was helpful to them as a model of progression which informed the sequencing of children's work and aided their thinking about where children should be going next. Although many teachers relied on their own experience for this, they found the levels helpful in backing up their decisions. The levels structure was, in some cases, making teachers more aware of children's attainment, with children at the ends of the attainment range being mentioned particularly. A Key Stage 3 Head of Department described how the department's scheme of work had been designed to address a range of attainment levels.

'And they follow, as I said, mostly the stranding that's been done for us, so we've kept it to those, but because of the nature of the kids we've got, I mean, in Year 9 we go mostly ... [...]... between levels 3 and 5, with ... obviously there's a rider that's right at the front of this saying ... that if your class is pushing on, don't for god's sake ... stop at level 5, that kind of thing ... you know, if you can push on beyond that, that's fine ... Year 8 goes right the way down to ... in some cases ... level one ... especially number work.'

In some cases the levels had encouraged teachers to push on with their higher attaining children, and they had become more aware of what to provide for the lower attaining children. Other comments included a reference to tightening up on planning. Children working through schemes and failing to reach the National Curriculum level appropriate to their attainment was mentioned as a problem. A Year 3 teacher, taking about the levels structure, said:

'It's made me rethink what I do with them, and certainly I try now to ... but you see, this is where the dilemma comes in ... because if they work their way through all these SCHEME books ... they don't get anywhere near the National Curriculum levels that are expected of them ...'

The teacher groups reported several areas in which the 10 level scale was helpful: in identifying pupils' levels of attainment; in planning for progression; in providing a common language for teachers to discuss pupils' progress and in providing an objective rather than a comparative framework for reporting on pupils' progress. They also felt that curriculum leaders found the levels useful in monitoring progress within a school.

The teachers interviewed for the NCC Maths Evaluation Project varied in the extent to which they were familiar with the 10 level structure and therefore in the extent to which they could comment upon the levels in any detail. Several teachers, particularly at KS3 related children's attainment to commercial scheme levels rather than NC levels, but some teachers were thinking of children in their class as at, or around certain NC levels. Some doubts were expressed about the advisability of categorising a child at a single level within a particular subject, because children were frequently at one level for one attainment target in mathematics, but at a different level for another. Categorising by NC level could disadvantage bi-lingual children, it was thought. One or two teachers were concerned about children's feelings of inadequacy when they saw their position on a 10 level scale, or remained at the same level for a long period of time.

No teacher in interview voiced major dissatisfaction with the 10 level scale - criticisms were relatively minor. Some teachers were anxious about what they perceived as gaps between levels, mainly between Level 1 and Level 2. Discrepancies between the difficulty of certain concepts placed at the same level were identified by the teacher groups and they thought that these should be addressed. It was felt that the SoAs in levels might not really reflect appropriate progression, in that not all were of the same demand and were, in some cases, vague and needed further exemplification. The current examples were not necessarily helpful. There was therefore a need for flexibility in interpretation. The levels fitted well, in the main, with schemes of work built up by interview teachers over years of teaching. One group of advisers consulted for the project had noted an improvement in the communication of attainment between Key Stages, with teachers becoming more aware of the wide range of attainment on intake.

It was felt by the teacher groups who had concentrated on a detailed study of the 1991 Order over two years, that although a 10 level scale was appropriate for assessment in that it helped teachers to appreciate the overall development of the curriculum over the full range of compulsory schooling, the levelled nature of the programmes of study did not form an adequate basis for planning teaching. The levelled PoS should be replaced by a key stage programmes of study which could be used as a basis for writing schemes of work and thus developing a coherent curriculum. Teachers needed to be given 'permission' to use their professional judgement when engaging in this activity.

• the 10 levels should be retained, with some attention being paid to address discrepancies which have been identified. There is a need for careful consideration of alternative presentations of the PoS within and across Key Stages.

3. Testing Arrangements?

There was evidence of the effects of assessment at the time of the interviews in Spring/Summer 1992 even though questions could not be asked directly by an NCC team on this aspect of the implementation of the National Curriculum.

Some teachers at Key Stages 1 and 2 were expressing anxieties about how to judge a child's understanding, and felt the need for exemplification of the SoAs. They also recognised the time needed to conduct Teacher Assessment properly. Positive feedback from the 1991 SATs, in which children were involved in extended practical activities, included an increased awareness of some children's levels of understanding, and an appreciation of ways of working to implement Ma1. Teachers had also felt the need to broaden the curriculum in some areas, or change the order in which they taught certain parts of the curriculum.

At Key Stage 3, the audit had focused attention on Ma1, and teachers were reporting the need to increase both quantity and quality of work involving using and applying mathematics. Teachers at this key stage also expressed a need for exemplification, requesting direction on different ways of assessing and marking the assessments. The introduction of the SATs had led some schools to devise their own assessment tasks for other areas of mathematics. Concerns about bi-lingual children being disadvantaged were expressed at both primary and secondary level.

The teacher groups were concerned that the definition of an SoA was becoming what a SAT writer said it was, with teachers not relying on their own wider interpretations. Further, there was uncertainty over the role of TA and SATs and, as noted above, how a final level was determined. If, due to current SAT practice of timed written tests, the SATs are taken to give meaning to broadly based or vague SoAs, this will lead to a narrowing of the curriculum. This points to the importance of TA in all key stages in more than Ma1.

4. SCAA?

Advice from the teacher groups was that early years specialists should be brought onto review bodies.

Thought should be given to streamlining documentation. Decisions about quality, timeliness and accompanying support should be carefully thought through, and enough time given to preparation and trialling. Consideration should be given to the pacing of documentation, so that teachers/departments/schools could have time to reflect on implementation.

It is also the case that some documentation might be better provided centrally, rather than at local level, eg recording documents.

REFERENCES

Alexander, R., Rose, J. and Woodhead, C. (1992) *Curriculum Organisation and Classroom Practice in Primary Schools*. London: HMSO.

Apple, M. (1992) Do the standards go far enough? Power, policy and practice in mathematics education. *Journal for Research in Mathematics Education*, Vol. 23, no. 5, pp. 413–31.

APU (1985) *A Review of Monitoring in Mathematics 1978–1982 Parts 1 and 2*. London: DES.

ASE/ATM/MA/NATE (1989) *The National Curriculum – Making it Work for the Primary School*. Hatfield: ASE.

ASE/ATM/MA/NATE (1990) *Teacher Assessment – Making it Work for the Primary School*. Hatfield: ASE.

ASE/ATM/MA/NATE (1992) *The National Curriculum – Making it Work at Key Stage 2*. Hatfield: ASE.

Askew, M., Brown, M., Johnson, D.C., Millett, A., Prestage, S. and Walsh, A. (1993) *Evaluation of the Implementation of National Curriculum Mathematics at Key Stages 1, 2 and 3. Volume 1: Report. Volume 2: Appendix*. London: SCAA.

Barrs, M. (1994) The road not taken. *Forum*, Vol. 36, no. 2, pp. 36–39.

Bauersfeld, H. (1979) Research related to the mathematical learning process. In *New Trends in Mathematics Teaching (Vol. 4)*, prepared by the International Commission on Mathematical Instruction. Paris: UNESCO.

Bassford, D. (1988) Fractions: A comparison of teaching methods. Nottingham: Shell Centre for Mathematical Education, University of Nottingham.

Bliss, J., Monk, M. and Ogborn, J. (1983) *Qualitative Data Analysis for Educational Research*. London: Croom Helm.

Booth, L.R. (1984) *Algebra: Children's Strategies and Errors*. Windsor: NFER-Nelson.

Bowe, R., Ball, S.J. and Gold, A. (1992) *Reforming Education and Changing Schools: Case Studies in Policy Sociology*. London: Routledge.

Brown, M. (ed.) (1992a) *Graded Assessment in Mathematics (GAIM)*. Walton-on-Thames: Nelson.

Brown, N. (1992b) Elaborate nonsense? The muddled tale of standard assessment tasks in mathematics at Key Stage 3. In C. Gipps (ed.) *Developing Assessment for the National Curriculum* (Bedford Way Series). London: Kogan Page.

Brown, S. (1980) *What Do They Know?* Edinburgh: HMSO.

Burkhardt, H., Fraser, R. and Ridgway, J. (1990) The dynamics of curriculum change. In I. Wirszup and R. Streit (eds) *Developments in School Mathematics Education Around the World (Vol. 2)*. Proceedings of the UCSMP International Conference on Mathematics Education, 1988. Reston, VA: NCTM.

CATS (1990) *Cats Mathematics Key Stage 3 Trial 1990 Report*. London: Consortium for Assessment and Testing in Schools, King's College.

CATS (1991) *Cats Mathematics Key Stage 3 Trial 1991 Report*. London: Consortium for Assessment and Testing in Schools, King's College.

CATS (1992) *Cats Mathematics Key Stage 3 Trial 1992 Report*. London: Consortium for Assessment and Testing in Schools, King's College.

Cockcroft, W.H. (1982) *Mathematics Counts: Report of the Committee of Inquiry into the Teaching of Mathematics in Schools*. London: HMSO.

Codd, J.A. (1988) The construction and deconstruction of educational policy documents. *Journal of Education Policy*, Vol. 3, no. 3, pp. 235–47.

Cox, C.B. and Dyson, A.E. (eds) (1969) *Fight for Education*. London: Critical Quarterly Society.

Daugherty, R. (1995) *National Curriculum Assessment: A Review of Policy 1987–1994*. London: Falmer.

Dearing, R. (1993) *The National Curriculum and its Assessment: Interim Report*. London: SEAC/NCC.

Dearing, R. (1994) *The National Curriculum and its Assessment: Final Report – December 1993*. London: SCAA.

Denvir, B. and Brown, M. (1986) Understanding of number concepts in low attaining 7–9 year olds: I and II. *Educational Studies in Mathematics*, Vol. 17, pp. 15–36 and 143–64.

Denvir, B., Brown, M. and Eve, P. (1987) *Attainment Targets and Assessment in the Primary Phase: Report of the Mathematics Feasibility Study*. London: King's College.

DES (1977a) *Education in Schools: A Consultative Document* (green paper). London: HMSO.

DES (1977b) *Circular 14/77: Local Authority Arrangements for the School Curriculum*. London: HMSO.

DES (1977c) *Curriculum 11–16. Working Papers by HMI*. London: HMSO.

DES (1979) *Local Authority Arrangements for the School Curriculum*. London: HMSO.

DES (1980a) *A Framework for the School Curriculum*. London: HMSO.

DES (1980b) *A View of the Curriculum*. London: HMSO.

DES (1983) Circular No. 8/83: *The School Curriculum*. London: HMSO.

DES (1985) *Mathematics from 5 to 16*. London: HMSO.

DES (1987) *National Curriculum Mathematics Working Group: Interim Report*. London: DES.

DES (1989) *National Curriculum: From Policy to Practice*. London: DES.

DES/APU (1980a) *Mathematics Development, Primary Survey Report No. 1*. London: HMSO.

DES/APU (1980b) *Secondary Survey Report*. London: HMSO.

Desforges, C. and Cockburn, A. (1987) *Understanding the Mathematics Teacher – A Study of Practice in First Schools*. London: Falmer.

DES/HMI (1979) *Mathematics 5–11: A Handbook of Suggestions*. London: HMSO.

DES/HMI (1983) *Curriculum 11–16: Towards a Statement of Entitlement*. London: HMSO.

DES/HMI (1984) *English for 5 to 16 (Curriculum Matters 1)*. London: HMSO.
DES/HMI (1985) *The Curriculum for 5–16 (Curriculum Matters 2*. London: HMSO.
DES/WO (1985) *Better Schools* (Cmnd 9469). London: HMSO.
DES/WO (1987) *National Curriculum Task Group on Assessment and Testing (TGAT)*. London: HMSO.
DES/WO (1988) *Mathematics for Ages 5 to 16 (Proposals of the Secretary of State for Education and Science and the Secretary of State for Wales)*. London: HMSO.
DES/WO (1989a) *Mathematics in the National Curriculum*. London: HMSO.
DES/WO (1989b) *Mathematics in the National Curriculum. Non-Statutory Guidance.* London: HMSO.
DES/WO (1991) *Mathematics in the National Curriculum (1991)*. London: HMSO.
DfE (1993) Final report on the National Curriculum and its assessment – the government response. Loose insert accompanying Dearing (1994).
DfE (1995) *Mathematics in the National Curriculum*. London: HMSO.
Dowling, P. and Noss, R. (1990) *Mathematics versus the National Curriculum.* Basingstoke: Falmer.
Ernest, P. (1991) *The Philosophy of Mathematics Education*. Basingstoke: Falmer.
Flanders, J.R. (1987) How much of the content in mathematics textbooks is new? *Arithmetic Teacher*, Vol. 35, no. 1, pp. 18–23.
Fowler, W.S. (1988) *Towards the National Curriculum*. London: Kogan Page.
Gipps, C., Brown, M., McCallum, B. and McAlister, S. (1995) *Intuition or Evidence? Teachers and National Assessment of Seven Year Olds*. Buckingham: Open University Press.
Gipps, C. and Goldstein, H. (1983) *Monitoring Children: An Evaluation of the Assessment of Performance Unit*. London: Heinemann.
Glaser, B.G. and Strauss, A.L. (1967) *The Discovery of Grounded Theory: Strategies for Qualitative Research*. Chicago, IL: Aldine.
Graham, D. with Tytler, D. (1993) *A Lesson for Us All: the Making of the National Curriculum*. London: Routledge.
Grouws, D., Good, T. and Dougherty, B. (1990) Teacher conceptions about problem solving and problem solving instruction. In G. Booker, P. Cobb and T. de Mendicuti (eds) *Proceedings of the Fourteenth International Conference for the Psychology of Mathematics Education*. Oaxtapec, Mexico: Programme Committee.
Harrison, A. (1982) *Review of Graded Tests (Schools Council Examinations Bulletin 41)*. London: Methuen Educational.
Hart, K. (ed.) *Children's Understanding of Mathematics: 11–16*. London: John Murray.
Hart, K. (1984) *Ratio: Children's Strategies and Errors*. Windsor: NFER-Nelson.
Haviland, J. (ed.) (1988) *Take Care, Mr Baker*. London: Fourth Estate.
HMI (1977a) *Mathematics, Science and Modern Languages in Maintained Schools in England*. London: HMSO.
HMI (1977b) *Curriculum 11–16*. London: HMSO.
HMI (1991a) *Mathematics Key Stages 1 and 3. A Report by HM Inspectorate on the First Year 1989–1990*. London: HMSO.
HMI (1991b) *Education Observed: The Implementation of the Curricular Requirements of ERA. An Overview by HM Inspectorate on the First Year, 1989–90*. London: HMSO.
HMI (1992a) *Mathematics Key Stages 1, 2 and 3. A Report by HM Inspectorate on the Second Year, 1990–91*. London: HMSO.
HMI (1992b) *Education Observed: The Implementation of the Curricular Requirements of ERA. An Overview by HM Inspectorate on the Second Year, 1990–91*. London: HMSO.
Hofkins, D. (1994) More numbers at the very start. *The Times Educational Supplement*, 13 May, p. iii.
Howson, G. (1988) *Maths Problem: Can More Pupils Reach Higher Standards?* London: Centre for Policy Studies.

Jaworski, B. (1994) *Investigating Mathematics Teaching: A Constructivist Enquiry.* London: Falmer.

Johnson, D.A. and Rising, G.R. (1972) *Guidelines for Teaching Mathematics.* Belmont, CA: Wadsworth.

Johnson, D.C. (ed.) (1989) *Children's Mathematical Framework 8–13: A Study of Classroom Teaching.* Windsor: NFER-Nelson.

Kerslake, D. (1986) *Fractions: Children's Strategies and Errors.* Windsor: NFER-Nelson.

Lawton, D. (1994) *The Tory Mind on Education 1979–94.* London: Falmer.

Lerman, S. (1990) Changing focus in the mathematics classroom. Paper presented at the eighth meeting of the Group for Research into Social Perspectives of Mathematics Education. London: South Bank University.

Lerman, S. (1993) The role of the teacher in children's learning of mathematics. In *Significant Influences on Children's Learning of Mathematics (Science and Technology Education Document Series No. 47).* Paris: UNESCO.

Lockheed, M.E., Vail, S.C. and Fuller, B. (1986) How textbooks affect achievement in developing countries: evidence from Thailand. *Educational Evaluation and Policy Analysis,* Vol. 8, no. 4, pp. 379–92.

Miles, M.B. and Huberman, A.M. (1984) *Qualitative Data Analysis.* Beverly Hills, CA: Sage.

Miwa, T. (1991) School mathematics in Japan and the US: focusing on recent trends in elementary and lower secondary school. In I. Wirszup and R. Streit (eds) *Developments in School Mathematics Education Around the World, Volume Three.* Reston, VA: NCTM.

NCC (1988) *Mathematics in the National Curriculum (A Report to the Secretary of State for Education and Science on the Statutory Consultancy for Attainment Targets and Programmes of Study in Mathematics).* York: NCC.

NCC (1991) *Report on Monitoring the Implementation of the National Curriculum Core Subjects 1989–1990.* York: NCC.

NCC (1992) *Using and Applying Mathematics, Books A and B.* York: NCC.

NFER/BGC (1991) *National Curriculum Assessment at KS1: 1991 Evaluation. A Report on the Working of the Standard Assessment Task.* Slough: NFER-BGC Consortium.

NFER/BGC (1992) *An Evaluation of the 1992 National Curriculum Assessment at Key Stage 1 in the Core Subjects.* Slough: NFER-BGC Consortium.

Nias, J., Southworth, G. and Campbell, P. (1992) *Whole School Curriculum Development in the Primary School.* London: Falmer.

Ofsted (1993a) *Curriculum Organisation and Classroom Practice in Primary Schools. A Follow-Up Report.* London: DfE.

Ofsted (1993b) *The Teaching and Learning of Number in Primary Schools. National Curriculum Mathematics Attainment Target 2.* London: HMSO.

Ofsted (1993c) *Mathematics Key Stages 1, 2 and 3. Third Year 1991–1992. A Report from the Office of Her Majesty's Chief Inspector of Schools.* London: HMSO.

Ofsted (1993d) *The Management and Provision of Inservice Training Funding by the Grant for Education Supply and Training (GEST). A Report from the Office of Her Majesty's Chief Inspector of Schools.* London: HMSO.

OU (1991) *Supporting Primary Mathematics. Handling Data.* Milton Keynes: Open University Press.

Parliamentary Expenditure Committee (1977) *The Attainment of the School Leaver.* London: HMSO.

Popham, W.J. (1969) Objectives and instruction. In W.J. Popham, E.W. Eisner, H.J. Sullivan and L.L. Tyler (eds) *Instructional Objectives (AERA Monograph).* Washington, DC: Rand McNally.

Prais, S. and Wagner, K. (1985) *Schooling Standards in Britain and West Germany.* London: National Institute of Economics and Social Research.

Robitaille, D.F. and Garden, R.A. (eds) (1989) *The IEA Study of Mathematics II: Contexts and Outcomes of School Mathematics.* Oxford: Pergamon Press.

SCAA (1994) *Mathematics in the National Curriculum. Draft Proposals.* London: HMSO.

Schmidt, W.H., Porter, A.C., Floden, R.E., Freeman, D.J. and Schwille, J.R. (1987) Four patterns of teacher content decision-making. *Journal of Curriculum Studies,* Vol. 19, pp. 439–55.

Schools Council (1965) *Curriculum Bulletin No. 1. Primary Mathematics.* London: HMSO.

SEAC (1992) *The Evaluation of National Curriculum Assessment at Key Stage 1 (1991). ENCA Project.* London: SEAC.

SEC (1985a) *Report of Working Party – Mathematics – Draft Grade Criteria.* London: SEC.

SEC (1985b) *National Criteria in Mathematics for the General Certificate of Secondary Education.* London: HMSO.

Sharma, S.S. (1993) *Graphs: Children's Strategies and Errors.* London: King's College.

Shuard, H., Walsh, A., Goodwin, J. and Worcester, V. (1990) *Children, Mathematics and Learning (Primary Initiative in Mathematics Education).* London: Simon & Schuster (for NCC).

Skemp, R. (1976) *Psychology of Learning Mathematics.* Harmondsworth: Penguin Books.

Spradley, J.P. (1979) *The Ethnographic Interview.* New York: Holt, Rinehart & Winston.

Strauss, A.L. (1987) *Qualitative Analysis for Social Scientists.* Cambridge: Cambridge University Press.

West Sussex Institute of HE Mathematics Centre (1987) *Better Mathematics: A Curriculum Development Study Based on the Low Attainers in Mathematics Inquiry.* London: HMSO.

Zhang, D. (1991) Some puzzling questions arising from mathematics education in China. In I. Wirszup and R. Streit (eds) *Developments in School Mathematics Education Around the World, Volume Three.* Reston, VA: NCTM.

INDEX